THE
Butterfly
Flies

EVA L. SHAW

ISBN 978-1-64079-930-1 (paperback)
ISBN 978-1-64079-931-8 (digital)

Christian Faith Publishing, Inc.
832 Park Avenue
Meadville, PA 16335
www.christianfaithpublishing.com

Disclaimer: Eva L Shaw is writing from her own experiences. Your experience may be different. It is her intent to keep confidences out of respect of all, including clients, friends, and family; therefore, real names are not used, and some experiences are changed slightly in order to maintain confidentiality. All poetry, unless otherwise stated, was written by Dr. Eva L. Shaw. Other writer's work is noted to the best of her ability to give proper credit. Opinions expressed are for information only. Seek professional help to explore your personal, physical, emotional, and spiritual needs. This document is not a diagnostic tool.

Printed in the United States of America

"I embrace emerging experience. I participate in discovery. I am a butterfly. I am not a butterfly collector. I want the experience of a butterfily"

—William Stafford

Written for those who are finding their way in life, those who help guide and support me on my journey, those who walked with me through trials and victories, those I have worked alongside, and last but not least, the clients who have courageously shared their stories of hurt, pain, and victory—I am forever grateful!

Dedicated to my mother, Edna Viola Smith. She passed away July 12, 2017, at the age of 96 years, just before 'The Butterfly Flies' was published. She was an accomplished and gifted poet and was in the International Poetry Hall of Fame. She wrote and published four books. She was a compassionate and caring individual and practiced forgiveness routinely. She was my example of a Christian life and I learned so much from her. She daily prayed for me and my family. Her strength will be missed. The memories are cherished forever.

(Inspiration for the book comes from
the story of the butterfly.)

I love a butterfly for all it gives to me
Amazing how it is created, an egg,
caterpillar to butterfly
I love a butterfly for what it gives our world
A chrysalis symbolizes a time of
change, great change
I love a butterfly, created all beautiful
The wings must dry and gain
strength first to become able
I love a butterfly as it flies away after rest
Free, beautiful, a gift from God
above—the butterfly.

—Eva L. Shaw, PhD, RCC, DCC

Contents

Biographical Sketch

Eva L. Shaw is the director of Make Life Happen Counselling and Coaching in Edmonton, Alberta, Canada. Eva believes that if you want the best out of life, then you are responsible to make your life happen. She counsels, mentors, writes, is an author, and a conference speaker. She is a veteran clinical counsellor and self-sabotage coach. As a Type 1 diabetic for over fifty-nine years, she knows the meaning of discipline and the hardship of living with a chronic disease.

Always persevering, Eva is a woman of character and high esteem. She makes it well-known that she is a wife and mother first and also a professional counsellor who teaches and mentors from a place of experience. She reiterates that as she lived her life, she then studied about it in books, which opened the door to learning about herself, her circumstances, and situations. Her purpose and calling since the age of twelve was, and continues to be, to spread the good news of *life*, with a hope that is everlasting. The exceptional gifts of empathy and teaching come from an outpouring of who she is on the inside. She has the heart of a counsellor. Her personal pain and release from it has made her a storyteller, and this is a read you will not forget. Her life is filled with the good, the bad, and the ugly. She likes to focus on the good, as there is much good spiritually, emotionally, and physically in her life. Her message to you is to enjoy the writing, cry with her, be with her, love with her, and find peace and joy *with her*.

Eva was born in a small town in Southwestern Ontario, Canada. She is proud to be a farmer's daughter. Her mother was a secretary in their hometown. Her mother, at the time of writing, is ninety-five years old. She has published several books of poetry and reads them to anyone who will listen! With little education, her father became a farmer because the war and the depression had left the family poor and her grandfather, a veteran, in ill health. The farm was the only source of income at that time.

At the age of seven, Eva was diagnosed with a life-threatening disease, juvenile diabetes, and wasn't expected to live a long life. Remember, Eva has had the disease for over fifty-nine years now. Life was kind of grim in those days. Public school, grades 1 to 8, was in a little brick schoolhouse with around eighteen pupils at any one time and then onto a bigger school and a three-hour bus ride each day to high school, grades 9 to 12. Upon graduation, Eva worked in a bank and soon married her high school sweetheart. Two babies arrived in the next five years, and a whole new world opened.

Many years later, Make Life Happen was coined as her counselling and coaching practice name. It is an expression of over thirty years' experience in the field of social work and clinical counselling, including her personal journey of failures and success.

The mission is to teach and walk beside those who have the desire to mature spiritually, emotionally, and physically. She is a storyteller and will share her wisdom and experiences. Some of her life experience is sad, but you will find this book is about the outcome and how she got there. Today Eva isn't sad; she is glad. She has lived a good life and is thankful, grateful, and joyful. Read on and you will see why this is.

To young people, Eva would tell you to realize you don't know what tomorrow will bring and that your choices bring results and outcomes. As you will see, she made some bad, in fact, terrible choices that brought heartache and pain not only to herself but also to others. Hindsight is wonderful, but foresight is better, as you can sometimes save yourself much pain. Learn from your elders, grandma and grandpa, mom and dad, adults who have lived life to its fullest; learn from their maturity. Don't think you know everything at your age; learn from others.

To the hurting, she would say, be grateful for the day, notice the small things in life, go for walks, get a pet that will love you unconditionally, find a counsellor who can maintain confidentiality and guide you on your road to healing. There is help, there is victory.

What is perseverance? One definition is "courage stretched out." It is about enduring and overcoming difficult circumstances with hope and joy. She believes that if we don't learn to persevere through struggles, we will simply give up. When we persevere, until we come out the other side, we grow stronger and develop greater confidence. We are of great value in life, unique in our own way, and each of us is a masterpiece.

She will tell you the story of the butterfly and how it relates to her journey. You see, the butterfly begins as an egg on a leaf, becomes a caterpillar who spins a chrysalis, and soon a beautiful butterfly emerges. She likes to compare each of these stages to her life.

Eva often has pictures come to her mind when counselling and when in prayer. It is a way that God speaks to and through her. So one day, during a particularly difficult and lonely time, she was praying. Into her view, like a vision, came a leaf—a beautiful green leaf. A caterpillar crawled up onto the leaf, the chrysalis was developed, and quickly a butterfly was sitting on the leaf drying its wings. The thought came: you are the butterfly drying your wings, and soon *you* will fly.

Eva's purpose in writing this book is to help folks understand that adversity in life is the journey in life. Remember, you are a person with a soul, spirit, and body. Personal growth brings success. We sometimes think we don't deserve good things in life. Even in the dark places, there is a light that shines, and we must find it. She had to train herself up with trial and error, making many mistakes. As you read her story, you will see success in education and a weakness in relationships that has brought her to her knees and helped her work with couples and with separation and divorce issues. Eva has lived it, educated about life and gone forth with excellence. Eva learned to raise her deserve level, and you can too.

As we travel through life, each of us has a story to tell, and to the best of her ability, she will tell you hers.

Eva says, "I hope you enjoy, cry, rejoice with me, and, at the end of it all, feel hope and security in your life and that you too can say, 'To God be the glory, great things He has done.'"

Chapter One

THE BUTTERFLY

"Life is an opportunity—benefit from it.
Life is beauty—admire it.
Life is bliss—taste it.
Life is a dream—realize it.
Life is a challenge—meet it.
Life is a duty—complete it.
Life is a game—play it.
Life is costly—care for it.
Life is wealth—keep it.
Life is love—enjoy it.
Life is a mystery—know it.
Life is a prize—fulfil it."

—Mother Theresa

A letter from Eva to all who think they cannot make it in life because life is just too tough:

I say to you, yes, you can, yes, you can, yes, you can! Just like the childhood story, *The Little Engine That Could*, when he said, "I think I can"—over and over again—until he accomplished the job. Then he finally said, "I thought I could, I thought I could." One step at a time, always looking up, looking ahead, and persevering—*yes, you can!*

This is my personal invitation to read my story. I hope my journey of times of despair, joy, and victory will come together to uplift and encourage you wherever you are in your life. Maybe your read will only be for curiosity or information alone. Then please take your knowledge and help someone else. Pass it on!

Let me tell you, I know the agony of having a lifelong chronic disease. I have experienced the joy of my children and the long exhausting nights when they were ill and wondering how I would make it through. I know the joy of marriage and the devastation of divorce as well as the exile of a child. And then there was the exhaustion and privilege of attending university and seminary and so much more.

Please take my hand as we have conversation about life.

Today is a day I will share with you writings of others that have influenced my life. The first one is one of my favorite author's works, Virginia Satir. It is called "My Declaration of Self-esteem." Through the years, I have read this over and over again and continue to do so. I give it to my clients. It is so full of truth. Please read and enjoy as we, together, enter the storytelling of my life.

"My Declaration of Self-esteem"
By Virginia Satir
American Author and Psychotherapist
1916–1988

I AM ME
In all the world, there is no one
else exactly like me—
Everything that comes out of me
is authentically mine,
Because I alone choose it—I own
everything about me—
My body, my feelings, my mouth,
my voice, all my actions
Whether they be to others or to myself—
I own my fantasies, my dreams,
my hopes, my fears—
I own all my triumphs and successes,
all my failures and mistakes.
Because I own all of me, I can become
intimately acquainted with me—
By so doing I can love me and be
friendly with me in all my parts—
I know there are aspects about
myself that puzzle me,
And other aspects that I do not know—

But, as long as, I am friendly and loving to myself,
I can courageously and hopefully look
for solutions to the puzzles
And for ways to find out more about me—
However, I look and sound whatever I say and do,
And whatever I think and feel at a given
moment in time is authentically me—
If later some parts of how I looked, sounded,
thought and felt turned out to be unfitting,
I can discard that which I feel is unfitting,
keep the rest, and invent something new
For which I discarded—
I can see, hear, feel, think, say, and do.
I have the tools to survive, to be close
to others, to be productive,
And to make sense and order out of the world
of people and things outside of me—
I own me, and therefore I can engineer me—
I am me and
I AM OKAY

And now here is the Butterfly Story, author unknown:

A man found a cocoon of a butterfly. One day, a small opening
appeared. He sat and watched
the butterfly for several hours as it
struggled to force its body through
that little hole. Then it seemed
to stop making any progress. It
appeared as if it had gotten as far as
it could, and it could go no further.

So the man decided to help the butterfly. He took a pair of scissors and snipped off the remaining bit of the cocoon. The butterfly then emerged easily, but it had a swollen body and small, shriveled wings.

The man continued to watch the butterfly because he expected that, at any moment, the wings would enlarge and expand to be able to support the body, which would contract in time. Neither happened! In fact, the butterfly spent the rest of its life crawling around with a swollen body and shriveled wings. It was never able to fly.

What the man, in his kindness and haste, did not understand was that the restricting cocoon and the struggle required for the butterfly to get through the tiny opening were God's way of forcing fluid from the body of the butterfly into its wings so that it would be ready for flight once it achieved its freedom from the cocoon.

> Sometimes struggles are exactly what we need in our lives. If God allowed us to go through our lives without any obstacles, it would cripple us. We would not be as strong as what we could have been. We could never fly!

I thought we might like to have some information about the metamorphosis that happens, so I went to the Internet and retrieved some of the following information from the Web sites www.mindyourmind and www.prezi.com. I would encourage you to go to these sites for more information about the butterfly. It is fascinating! I summarize the applicable information.

A caterpillar is formed from the egg that is deposited on a leaf. Caterpillars have 4,000 muscles in their body, while the human has only 629. I remember, as a child, watching the caterpillar with yellow and black stripes crawl across the ground. Now I understand why they can do that so gracefully. It is because of the 4,000 muscles in their body. I would compare this to myself as a child who was not diagnosed as hyperactive; however, I have been told that I was extremely active and questioned everything with an inquisitive mind. The thoughts that must have been fleeting through this child's mind as I watched, waited, explored, and questioned. I can remember, from a very young age, when I was enamoured with thoughts, and life was a fairy tale to me.

Sometimes in life it is difficult to stay on the right track, and I got lost along the way. There were periods of time in my life when I suffered from depression, anxiety, and suicidal thoughts, and I struggled not to give up, just like the caterpillar who is building the cocoon. If you ever get a chance to watch the amazing work of the caterpillar, please take advantage, but do not disturb him, he is very focused on survival. Just like him, I have gone through processes in life to get to today.

The transformation from caterpillar to butterfly is called the pupa. In my life, the transformation took years and years. I had a lot to learn, and I had lots of questions I needed answers to. I live by "Seek and you will find." Each question I resolved took me to new heights, and like the caterpillar who came through the metamorphosis, I entered adulthood emotionally and spiritually.

The metamorphosis is a time of breaking out of the cocoon to become the butterfly and then sitting on a leaf to dry its wings. This was a time for me of wiggling, squirming, lots of anger, and asking, "Why me?" It was difficult; however, I came to understand that we are put in this world to live life, and that means learning and growing personally, and it sometimes felt like I was being pulled through a keyhole. I asked, "Why, God? Why me?" At the time when I had a picture come to my mind of me as a butterfly drying my wings on a leaf, getting ready to fly, I felt the weakness of the body and the strength of the fluid pouring into my wings to set me free. That strength was God in my spirit.

So let's look a little further. A butterfly has four different life stages. Stage one is the small egg that is laid by a female butterfly. It hatches into a caterpillar in five to ten days. The second stage is the larva or caterpillar, which is long and wormlike with pattern of patches or stripes! It starts to eat all the time. This is the growing stage. It sheds its skin or molts many times as it grows. Stage three is when the caterpillar changes into a pupa and attaches itself upside down to a twig! It sheds its last skin and grows a shell called a chrysalis. This is the resting and changing stage. It starts to turn into the butterfly. After about three weeks, it escapes from its chrysalis shell as an adult butterfly, and it pushes its legs out and frees its wings. The soft wings are folded against its body. The butterfly is tired, and so it rests to dry its wings. It will soon fly, but first it will pump blood into its wings. This will get them working and flapping. Now it must learn to fly. A butterfly cannot fly very well at first. It needs to practice; however, they do learn fast, so it doesn't take very long. It will then look for food, find a mate, and lay its eggs, and the life cycle stages start all over again.

Just some *fun* facts about butterflies (retrieved from but not quoted) http://www.tooter4kids.com/Life Cycle/fun_facts.html:

- Butterflies taste with their feet.
- Butterflies do not have mouths.

- Butterflies need sun to fly.
- Butterflies fly during the day.
- Butterflies can see some colors. They can see red, yellow, and green.
- Butterflies cannot fly if they are too cold. They need to be warm to fly.
- Butterflies have their skeleton on the outside of their body to protect them. It also keeps the water on the inside of their body so they don't dry out.
- The wings of a butterfly are transparent and have tiny scales. They give the wings color. This is why they do not look transparent to us.

I think butterflies are very unique, beautiful creatures that God created to bring us joy! How can one not feel joy and freedom when observing a butterfly flitting around the flowers? I just say, awesome to that!

Jeffrey Glassberg says it so well. "Beautiful and graceful, varied and enchanting, small but approachable, butterflies lead you to the sunny side of life. And everyone deserves a little sunshine."

On that day when the thought came to me of myself as a butterfly ready to fly, I thought, *Who? Me? Ready to fly?* I had been in great emotional pain, and so it seemed impossible. However, I said, I will watch this materialize because I want to fly. That was long ago now. When I look at myself today in comparison to then, I can truly say, yes, I am flying. That doesn't mean I am perfect, nor does it mean I do not make mistakes; it simply means I am doing things in life that I thought were impossible. You see, at the time, I had just left a relationship with a man who said he had no belief in God. While with him, I wasn't able to discuss my faith, nor did I attend a church of believers, and at the time, it was easier to just go along with him than stand up for what I believed in. I was alone and frightened when the thought came. I was very weak physically and spiritually. Emotionally, I was a wreck. So I questioned, *Lord, how will I fly? Where will I fly to? What is about to happen?* From that day on, things began to change. Change for me is never easy; just at the chrysalis stage is a struggle, I struggled through. So here is the story of the butterfly and the person.

A CHRONIC DISEASE STRIKES

"She liked being reminded of butterflies. She remembered being six or seven and crying over the fates of the butterflies in her yard after learning that they lived for only a few days. Her mother had comforted her and told her not to be sad for the butterflies, that just because their lives were short didn't mean they were tragic. Watching them flying in the warm sun among the daisies in their garden, her mother had said to her, see, they have a beautiful life. Alice liked remembering that."

—Lis Genova, *Still Alice*

"For with God, nothing shall be impossible."

—Luke 1:37

EVA L. SHAW

I was diagnosed with Type 1 diabetes at seven years of age. December 7 was the date, just a few days before Christmas. I became a seven-year-old with a monitored diet and no candy for Christmas. It was tough for me and the whole family.

A couple of years ago, I received the Joslin Institute medal for being a courageous diabetic for over fifty years, and I intend to get the next one at seventy-five years. At present time, it is a possibility, as my health is stable.

A diabetic must be as independent as possible. However, I believe it is a family disease. What about the times when blood sugar is so low that the person cannot help herself? Someone has to take the responsibility and help the person. You can call 911, get them to emergency at the hospital, or at least get them a snack—if they can eat it. There were many times as a child when I couldn't wake up in the morning. My parents had to deal with bringing me out of unconsciousness. I am a lucky one, I never was hospitalized with ketoacidosis. However, I was in hospital many times as a child and young adult with flu, ear infections, tonsillitis, and just a cold could throw the diabetes balance dangerously and quickly out of control.

The Mayo Clinic Staff Definition of ketoacidosis is "…a serious complication of diabetes that occurs when your body produces high levels of blood acids called ketones. The condition develops when your body can't produce enough insulin. Insulin normally plays a key role in helping sugar (glucose), a major source of energy in your muscles and other tissues, enter your cells. Without enough insulin, your body begins to break down fat as fuel. This process produces a buildup of acids in the bloodstream called ketones, eventually leading to diabetic ketoacidosis if untreated."

Being married or involved with a Type 1 diabetic can be a stressful time, as diabetes is a chronic endocrine gland system disease. It causes mood swings, sick days, trips to many doctors, high-risk pregnancy, and dependency, at times, on family and friends.

I really don't know how my young husband managed. We divorced after thirteen years of marriage. He did well with helping me with diabetes, and if I could, I would tell him that. My three pregnancies were high-risk, and I lost the first baby to miscarriage. We were told that we probably wouldn't be able to have children, but we tried again, and soon two beautiful boys were born. After the second, I made the decision not to have another child. Pregnancy was too risky for me and the baby. The pregnancies were tough, and the knowledge that the children could be diabetic, disfigured, deaf, or blind was always on my mind. My husband worked his new career with hours of taking me to the doctor and emergencies, like when I fell at seven months' pregnant. I think he had the patience of Job in those years. After a miscarriage and two children, I knew we had our family and was so grateful that the little ones were healthy.

I sometimes wonder how people around me deal with the mood swings from the diabetes. They happen at home, in the grocery store, at work, and anywhere I happen to be. My temperament and personality is soft-spoken, caring, and I try to be kind. I am more introverted than extroverted. However, when a low blood sugar "hits," I need time alone. I need what I need to raise the blood sugar, and arguing with me will only cause an explosion. I cannot be reasoned with—that is impossible. When my blood sugar is high, I feel sluggish, tired, and withdrawn. The swings in blood sugar are very hard to describe, but they can be like the Alberta weather—sunny one minute and raining the next, snow the next and blowing the next. I may be seen as unpredictable and just plain cocky at times. I try very hard to keep a good balance, but the brittle blood sugar seems to always be working against me. If I am under stress, okay, watch out.

After the divorce, with two young boys to raise, I accepted a position as the executive director of a woman's shelter. I got five years of management experience with very hard knocks. There wasn't enough money from government support to run the shelter, so fund-raising was a huge task. Because working with battered and abused women and their children is an emotionally charged population, and there is always a safety aspect to the work too, staff were stretched to their limit, and I was found to be mediator, supporter, and counsellor. The staff often rebelled, and that was very difficult. As part of my job, I was directed to take business management courses, and I achieved a two-year diploma. I attended workshops, college courses, night school, and weekend courses to achieve two one-year certificates in social work and child abuse. My vacation time was spent at university doing condensed education for three years. I know that my children suffered during these years. I hardly had time to think, let alone be present with them. I provided a nice new home, new car, and their basic needs, but I was unable to meet their emotional needs. The stress caused big problems with the diabetes, and I ended up in hospital several times. Probably my greatest regret with my children is how it seemed to them that I put them last, and everything else must have seemed to come first. In my mind, however, I was doing what I needed to do for my children. My son has since told me that I was a "monster mom" whom he was afraid of, but that I also could be kind and loving, and that was the mom he needed. He couldn't trust me to know which mom he was going to get. I think that analogy is true.

I wrote an article called "Diabetics in the Workplace." It is used to teach first year doctors and dentists at the University of Alberta. I hope it helps them to get a true picture of what it is like to live with diabetes. I hope you also get some real insight as you read it.

Diabetics in the Workplace

According to the Canadian Diabetes Association, "diabetes is a chronic disease in which the body either cannot produce insulin or cannot properly use the insulin it produces. Approximately nine million Canadians live with diabetes."

There are many diabetics in the workforce.

I am proud to say I received the Joslin Institute Award for living successfully with diabetes for over fifty years. It has been quite the journey. When I was diagnosed as a child of seven, it was a life-changing experience for my whole family. Overnight, there was panic and questions of the future. My mother, a stay-at-home mom, had to quickly get into the workforce, as we had no medical coverage, and hospital stays as well as insulin and treatments were very expensive. We quickly realized that exercise, such as riding a bicycle, would act in the body similar to insulin to reduce blood sugar levels, and that could quickly become a hypoglycemic reaction or too low blood sugar—threatening unconsciousness. As a teenager, the stress of hormonal changes, problems with "boyfriends," and wanting to be "the same as my peers" created issues such as eating proper foods at appropriate times and not "burning the candle at both ends." Emotional stressors affected blood sugar, making it go too high or too low, and writing exams could reflect either. Then onto the workplace, my first job was at age seventeen, and now I am in the last stage of my career. I can tell lots of stories about diabetes experiences as can my diabetic friends. Here are a few:

"So you are a diabetic, you must be *used* to needles." If you think about it, whoever could get *used* to having a needle? A diabetic endures needles because taking insulin is the only way to live. I can assure you I never got used to them, nor did I like them. I am fortunate now to have an insulin pump, which, in short, acts something like an artificial pancreas.

As for finger pricks, I prick my finger at least seven times a day and more if I am ill. This is to get a drop of blood to place in a little machine that gives me a blood glucose reading. From that reading, I figure out whether I need to eat or take insulin, or maybe I don't need to do either. Before eating, the reading tells me how much insulin I need to balance with the food I will eat…well, I have had folks say, "I guess that doesn't even hurt you anymore." Really? As a diabetic, I am not prone to pain? Well, my fingers get sore and calloused and look ugly, but I still have to prick them, or I could get very ill. It hurts me just as much as the next guy.

When going to some food events, I have had the hostess say to me, "I really should have made you something special because you are a diabetic." To say the least, this is embarrassing and unneeded. I know what I can eat, I know when I can eat, I know how much to eat, and I am the best judge of it all, as I know myself well. In fact, I can eat most foods. I have had much experience in the field of diabetes, and I have been trained by the best in the medical field, doctors, nutritionists, specialists, and experiencing diabetes is the *very* best teacher.

And then there is "Oh, I know all about diabetes. I have a relative who has it too," and then the person goes on to tell me all about diabetes. I politely listen, but in truth, we diabetics have our own unique stories, and each diabetic is very different, including the fact that there are several types of diabetes. Please don't put us all in the same box.

"I am having an event this weekend, but I didn't invite you because I know you could never do it due to your diabetes." Let me advise that diabetics, especially now with the insulin pump and other strategies, can do most anything anyone else can do, even skydive, and the diabetic really does know what they feel comfortable doing and are the best judge. So please don't leave us out!

"Oh, you are having another bad day." I have found that I cannot get through one week saying, "That was a terrific week," and this is why. Usually, two or more low blood sugar events occur in a month. This causes headache, shakiness, extreme hunger pangs, and an overall ill feeling—sometimes for a full day. And then there is the "fighting of the high blood sugars," which can be for many reasons, and sometimes just doesn't seem to have any reason at all. High blood sugar can cause long-term complications of neuropathy, retinopathy, heart attacks, strokes as well as other illnesses. Being diabetic is a twenty-four-hour watchfulness lifestyle...oh yeah, I have a low immune system, and so I get sick easily too. Working when not feeling 100 percent is common, as there are most days when a diabetic has events that usually no one else even knows about. It is sometimes difficult finding time to go to all the medical appointments that are necessary, the dentist, medical doctor appointments, endocrinologist, podiatrist, nutritionist, and so on. These are all medically needed appointments on a regular basis, and then when I get ill, the appointments increase. You see, illness of any kind, including the common cold, makes the blood sugar go all "whacky," and it is hard and tedious work to get it back into control as the body fights for rebalancing.

I have friends who are diabetics, and I asked them for a few of their experiences—we laughed together.

A diabetic of twenty-six years says, "I was in the break room at work today when a coworker of mine, who is concerned about some symptoms she's having, asked me if there is a test for diabetes. I explained to her how they can test for it and the symptoms." A guy coworker of two weeks said, "You bleed excessively when you get cut or injured." She was horrified. I sat there and let him go on to explain that if she was diabetic, this would be a tell-tale sign. I quipped, "So you mean when you have diabetes, you have excessive bleeding when injured?" and he very confidently said yes. I calmly challenged. "I don't know where you got your training, but that is not true." He asked, "And what school did you go to?" I replied, "The school of experiencing diabetes." End of conversation. (This was a story that was on Facebook. Anonymous.)

If you work with a diabetic, have one as a friend or are one, then here is my nutshell of thoughts for you:

If you work with a diabetic, be respectful of the knowledge that person has of their own health. Be willing to help and support, but don't be intrusive and do ask what the boundaries are.

As a friend or coworker, offering your support and asking for suggestions of what to do in an emergency or crisis is a good idea. Otherwise, don't worry if you happen to see the diabetic doing a finger prick or eating at an inopportune time or sitting back for a few minutes to wait for the blood sugar level to rise. I am just taking care of "me," and soon I will return to "normal."

As a diabetic, I learned that if I accept myself, others accept me too. However, there are times when I have my "feel sorry for myself" days too. I try to be respectful of others and know that their comments are coming from a place of helpfulness, helplessness, or ignorance. I use every chance I get as a teaching moment. I try not to overwhelm anyone with my comments, as diabetes is second nature to me but can be a new experience for others.

I am proud to say that I have lived with the diabetes lifestyle all these years, and I intend to put more years on the calendar. The Joslin Institute also gives a seventy-five-year award, and I would like to add it to my collection. I am a wife, mother, successful professional, and I am a diabetic. It is my lifestyle. Diabetes has never made life easy. My family, friends, medical team, and coworkers, all in their own way, help me on this journey called *life*.

Chapter Three

SEXUAL ABUSE

"So, come with me where dreams are born,
And time is never planned
Just think of happy things and
Your heart will fly on wings in
Never Never Land."

—Peter Pan

"We delight in the beauty of the butterfly, but rarely admit the changes it has
gone through to achieve that beauty."

—Maya Angelou

I am worthwhile—I struggled through the name-call-
ing and other things that caused me self-sabotage
issues as an adult. Please try to understand this poem

as I introduce sexual abuse and domestic violence issues.

A world of make belief
Daydreaming and imagery
A fairytale childhood
With protective loving parents,
Siblings who cared
Children and—
A perfect family plan.
This world is full of hurt and pain—
To love and to be loved
Hurt and despair.
So, not to go on with
A picture of remorse and regrets.
Grieving the past, but
One day I knew that
I am worthwhile.
I will go on. I have a purpose.
The struggles are not over
But I will go on.
Searching, oh searching,
'Prostitute' rang clear
'No one will ever want you'
'Ugly, stupid, useless.'
Someone, one day,
Helped me to see
I am worthwhile.
I will go on. I have a purpose.
My dreams one day I'll see.
The memories will fade and
I will be whole,

Able to live, in spite of it.
Is there any forgiveness?
I Am Worthwhile.

As a child and as a woman in our society, it is difficult to escape sexual abuse. I am in the statistics. I wrote my Ph.D. thesis, "Historic Female Childhood Sexual Abuse from a Christian Counsellor's Perspective." I researched and developed it as a manual to help Christian counsellors. I know the issue from experiencing it, studying it, and hearing countless stories from courageous women and men who have been victimized.

My desire in writing this book is not to share horrendous stories that may revictimize others but to bring some level of understanding to those who read it. In the end, I hope it brings encouragement and joy to your heart. It suffices to say that sexual abuse was a part of my life. RAINN (Rape, Abuse & Incest National Network) gives statistics that says every two minutes, an American is sexually abused. One out of every six women has been raped, attempted, or completed. Only six out of every one thousand rapists end up in prison. Please note that RAINN created and operates the National Sexual Assault Hotline, 800-656-HOPE.

Canadian Statistics Taken as information from the Web site, Sexual Assault.ca

A Numerical Representation of the Truth

- Of every 100 incidents of sexual assault, only 6 are reported to the police
- 1–2% of "date rape" sexual assaults are reported to the police
- 1 in 4 North American women will be sexually assaulted during their lifetime
- 11% of women have physical injury resulting from sexual assault
- Only 2–4% of all sexual assaults reported are false reports
- 60% of sexual abuse/assault victims are under the age of 17
- over 80% of sex crime victims are women
- 80% of sexual assault incidents occur in the home
- 17% of girls under 16 have experienced some form of incest
- 83% of disabled women will be sexually assaulted during their lifetime
- 15% of sexual assault victims are boys under 16
- half of all sexual offenders are married or in long-term relationships
- 57% of aboriginal women have been sexually abused
- 1/5 of all sexual assaults involve a weapon of some sort
- 80% of assailants are friends and family of the victim

The above noted statistics have been taken from various studies across Canada.

I do not care to name or tell my stories in detail. There was a time when I wanted to shout all the details from the rooftop and to expose the lurid details. However, as I have worked through my anger, come to a place of forgiveness and done what I could to confront the issue, I no longer have that desire. Everyone's experience with sexual abuse is different, as is the outcome. What is important is that the manifested feelings and symptoms are resolved.

What bothers me the most is that our society is still so accepting of it. Women and children still are not protected. Every time I locate statistics like this, I find them just staggering, and quite frankly, they make me angry!

The following letter written by Diane Hawkins indicates the writer is well acquainted with the damage caused and the effects of childhood sexual abuse. I could have written it myself, as it reflects my pain and those of all who have been sexually abused. Thank you, Diane Hawkins, for writing this so well. Here it is:

An open letter to child sexual abusers:
Dear Father,
    Stepfather,
        Grandfather,
            Brother,
                Uncle,

Babysitter,
    Neighbour,
        Whoever you are—

You who see that innocent child playing happily in her yard, lying peacefully in her bed—You who are tempted to suavely enter her private domain and take a little sexual joy for yourself, my heart cries to you from its deepest depths, 'Before you touch, please, please, please, oh, please, consider what damage you are inflicting upon her.'

'Just one time,' you say.

'She won't be aware, she's sleeping.'

'She's too young to even know that it's wrong.'

'She'll think we're playing.'

'I won't go all the way.'

'She needs to learn about sex.'

Yes, you have your excuses, your reasons, your alibis, but deep down you know that it's your own self-centered pleasure and the need to feel your power that lies at the heart of this lustful desire. Oh, selfish man, will you not realize that the power of love and self-control is by far the mightier sword to wield? It leaves no scars of guilt or shame or remorse— no scars on you and no scars on her. Scars are forever, my friend. The wounds may heal, but the scars never ever completely disappear. Do you really want to wound her? Do you really want her to bear the permanent scars of your selfish pleasure? What has she done, I ask you, what has she done to deserve such a destiny?

'You talk of wounds and scars and destiny,' I hear you say.

'I'm talking of only a touch, only a caress, only a feel. I do not mean to damage her.'

And that is just why I am writing to you. You do not know the depth of agony that touch, that caress, that feel will cause that child to bear. The fact that she has been betrayed by one in who she fearlessly put her love and trust will be too overwhelming for her to handle as a child. The reaction you see will be small, or even one of positive receptivity, as she drinks in the feeling of pseudo affection for which she has perhaps been starved, but don't you know that down the road, yes, down the road, some-day she will have to deal with this memory of violation and abuse? Sooner or later, she will know that those were hands that moved not in love for her, not in warm affection, but only for them-selves. They took; they did not give. They took that which was most precious to her, that which was to be hers alone.

And then the pain; the searing, tearing, tormenting pain; will wrench the very depths of her being—the pain of betrayal, the pain of humiliation and shame, the pain of being used instead of loved, exploited instead of pro-tected. And that pain won't last just a day nor just a week. It will go on for months and months, and perhaps even years as she resurrects those long-buried emotions, which she could never express as a child, those emotions that subtly continue to hold her life in dismal bondage. They will all need to come out in order for her ever to be set free from their power.

It will take much strength and courage on her part to walk the long, fiery road to healing, but if she doesn't, she will continue to be plagued by deep inner hostility, depression, psychosomatic illnesses and malfunctions in many areas of her life. It will undoubtedly affect her ability to relate to men in a healthy way. She will be caught between the extremes of fear and sexual frigidity, on the one hand, and promiscuity on the other, knowing how to relate to men only through sex, forever craving the true love and affection she never got as s child. She will have difficulty in forging deep, trusting relationships. Her enormous load of repressed anger will unexpectedly explode at inappropriate times and usually at those she loves the most. If she has children, she may be hindered in developing the normal intimacy of the parent-child relationship. She may even be inclined to mistreat them, thus continuing the cycle of abuse. In any case, the joy of motherhood will probably be much decreased for her as she battles feelings of inadequacy, guilt, self-hate, and depression. She will also be greatly predisposed to alcoholism and drug abuse, unconsciously trying to escape from the inner pain that haunts her so relentlessly.

These, my friend, are just a few of the damages she will suffer from your selfish act. Do you really want her to be marred in this way? Please, I beg you again, please consider these facts—

BEFORE YOU TOUCH!
Painfully written by One So Touched

Because of my experience of not being believed, I know it is difficult for some to understand flashbacks to a traumatic event. I decided to quote part of the article written by the University of Alberta Sexual Assault Center and published on their Web site. They are specialists in the area of abuse, and I appreciate their information on flashbacks as it is described so well.

COPING WITH FLASHBACKS

"Flashbacks are memories of past traumas. They may take the form of pictures, sounds, smells, body sensations, feelings, or the lack of them (numbness). Many times there is no actual visual or auditory memory with flashbacks. One may have a sense of panic, of being trapped, or a feeling of powerlessness with no memory stimulating it. These experiences can also happen in dreams. During the initial crisis, the survivor had to insulate herself/himself from the emotional and physical horrors of the trauma. In order to survive, that insulated part of the self remained isolated, unable to express the feelings and thoughts of that time. It is as though the survivor put that part of herself/himself into a time capsule, which later surfaces and comes out as a flashback, feeling just as intense in the present as it did during the crisis. When that part comes out, the survivor is experiencing the past as if it were happening today. The intense feelings and body sensations occurring are frightening because the feelings/sensations are not related to the reality of the present and many times seem to come from nowhere. The survivor may begin to think she/he is crazy and is afraid of telling anyone of these experiences. The survivor may feel out of control and at the mercy of her/his experiences. Flashbacks are unsettling and may feel overwhelming because the

51

survivor becomes so caught-up in the trauma that she/he forgets about the safety and security of the present moment."

I found it helpful, when I had flashbacks, to admit to myself that I am having a flashback. Reminding myself that it was "just" a memory from the past and that I survived it. I must say that the flashes of memory were scary, and it was hard to believe that this was happening to me. I thought I was going crazy. I felt like I was out of control. At first, I couldn't control what was happening and learned that I was having flooding memory. As time went on, I became able to control the flashbacks and work through them. I got to the place where I could tell myself, "This will pass." And it did.

1. I learned and practiced deep breathing because I would find that I would stop breathing or take very shallow breaths. Oxygen to the brain was needed to control the anxiety.

2. I had a stuffed toy rabbit that was my first baby toy. I still have him. I would hold him in my hands and just focus on him until I could "re-enter" real life. It was probably only minutes, but it felt like hours. Afterward, I was exhausted, and if possible, I would lie down and sleep. However, sometimes I was afraid to go to sleep in case I would have a nightmare, so I would go walking by the lake.

If you are going through this, then find what is comforting for you. The sound of the water and watching the waves come into shore are very healing for me, and I find peace there. I used to tell my kids, and they thought I was crazy, that "the water speaks to me." It truly felt that the water spoke healing into my heart.

3.   Sleeping was a way that I coped when I was a child. I would crawl up on my bed or my parents' bed and sleep. There was comfort there. Self-care is very important.

4.   If you have a friend or relative that you can talk to about the flashback and you feel safe with this person, then debriefing with them could be good. I had no one. I would write in my journal and talk to the counsellor. Sometimes I would talk in the group therapy, and most times I would just listen. I remember one group night we were asked to draw a picture of how we were feeling. I drew a red heart for angry and with a lightning flash cutting through the middle of the heart for brokenhearted. I remember feeling frozen as I did this drawing.

Frozenness sometimes happens to sexual abuse survivors. I experienced this when I felt vulnerable and threatened. All feelings would disappear, and I couldn't move, nor could I speak. I have learned that I was feeling so many feelings that I couldn't take it anymore, and I shut down. Mind and body became immobile.

5. Bring life back into balance. You must find your way to do this. I compare it to a teeter-totter that is balanced. When either end is high up to the sky or sitting on the ground, the teeter-totter is out of balance. I use this as my visual of our emotions. We must get grounded, we must balance again so we can go on with life.

6. I had to be patient with myself as I worked through this process. Healing takes time. It takes time to learn what you need to take care of yourself. A great book to read is *The Courage to Heal* by Ellen Bass and Laura David. I found it and the workbook a great help in my healing, and I have recommended it to many survivors.

The journey to healing is different for each of us. There is great grief and loss when childhood sexual abuse is present. I envision it as putting one foot in front of the other and just walking through it. Sexual abuse is a lifetime healing process, but it does get better.

Healing, when there are intrusive memories happening, feels like it is right up front in your face. The wounds are open, and the memories need to be healed and integrated into one's lifeline of events. Intrusive memories are when it seems as if the memories are in control. When healing has occurred, then we are in control of the memories, we can pull them up or just let them lie. They have no control of us any longer.

I suffered from flashbacks for several years. I compartmentalized as much as I could so I could continue to function. I had to, as I was a single mom with children. I was a mess emotionally and very fatigued. I worked and went to school and tried to keep a normal day routine. I was hospitalized twice. I was often flooded at work to the point where I had to shut my office door and write the memories as they came. I spent hours at home in my bedroom allowing the flashbacks to "play themselves out." I had many sleepless nights. Nightmares were routine. I sought counselling and attended individual and group sessions. Sharing this was very difficult.

When I look back on those years, I truly do not know how I managed to continue going on other than there is no other choice. I didn't always cope well and reacted with my children, and at work I became strong and aggressive. I put myself in harm's way often, not even thinking about my safety. I was executive director of a women's shelter and truly stood up for the clients, but then I had a visit from a kind policeman who pointed out how I was making their job difficult, trying to keep me safe. I was working for the safety of others by putting myself at risk. I wasn't courageous; I was risking my own life when others were willing to help.

Here is a poem I wrote during this time in my life!

"Torment"

Terror, torture, memories,
Confusion, bad times, good times,
I cannot understand it.
I am loved, but I feel hated,
I cannot trust myself or anyone,
A little child living in a state of torment.
I wondered, *Who am I?*

Part of me wanted to tell the world what I was experiencing, as this felt freeing. The other side of me was scared to tell anyone. I was afraid of judgment, and when I did tell, judgment did come.

Possibly, the memories were triggered by the divorce and possibly from hearing stories from the women I worked with who were trauma victims. It was a tough time for me, and along with the grief came the flashbacks. I struggled for probably a year with counselling and on my own, telling very few people. When I did tell, I was reminded of the False Memory Syndrome Foundation, and this made me go underground for quite some time. In fact, it perpetuated my move from Ontario to Alberta. I didn't want to be accused of lying, but I was. I believe this is a worry for many survivors. Could this be a reason we have trouble trusting? When we finally come to a place of telling, then people tell us we are lying.

People who come through war events and car accidents and other trauma tend to forget the incidents. In the case of war, there is no doubt that they were there and that the war happened. Incidents of childhood trauma have been described as similar in experience.

I think that not wanting to believe that others have been hurt, especially as children, is understandable—it isn't an easy thing to acknowledge. Just because it is hard to wrap our head around it doesn't mean it didn't happen. When people disbelieved me, I felt judged and belittled and angry. I took it to mean that they were calling me a liar. I could never understand why anyone would want to lie about something so horrific, but I guess it just meant that it was easier to call me a liar than to face the truth for themselves.

Yes, people do forget traumatic events, and yes, they do recover memories later on in life, usually when they are feeling safe to do so. People do forget overwhelming traumatic events, and for a child, this is the way they protect themselves. Sometimes there is no memory of the incidents or sometimes only partial memory. Someone who has been in a car accident but has no memory of it may have strong negative reactions when driving by the scene of an accident. A war veteran may jump when someone walks up behind them without understanding why; abuse survivors may do the same. This is called hypervigilance.

Kali Munro (2001), a psychotherapist from Toronto, wrote a paper entitled "Trusting Your

Memories of Child Abuse." She says, "We know that people forget traumatic events. We know that even without memories of the event, people have post-traumatic reactions even in relatively mild forms. We also know that memories once forgotten can return. Again, this has been documented with war veterans who initially forgot their war experiences and then remembered them later usually via spontaneous flashbacks."

I didn't tell people details of my flashbacks. For one reason, they didn't want to hear it, and for another, I knew I couldn't be certain of every single detail. However, I am confident that the crime of sexual abuse occurred, I know who did it, and I know my approximate age when it happened. An analogy that Kali Munro uses in her paper is of a bank robbery. The robbers have guns. People are afraid for their safety. Eyewitnesses often contradict each other about the details, but no one is uncertain about the fact that there was a robbery, and people were scared for their lives.

"A Reflection"

There once was a child
Filled with play,
Joyous and happy,
Beaming with light.
The world became dark.
For years a bleak place.
Sad and neglected,

THE BUTTERFLY FLIES

A sad, sorry sight.
As years came and went,
Troubled tumultuous and growth—
The happy little girl
Wanted to be part
Of the woman's life now.
But, still rejected by all,
Hide her we don't want her—
Be adult—we like you sad.
I won't hide I will be seen
One day to the world
And those who could have seen
Will regret not sharing
That little girl's life.
In reflection, I see her now.

Chapter Four

MARRIAGE

"We are like butterflies who flutter for a day and think it is forever."

—Carl Sagan

"I belong to my beloved, and his desire is for me. Come, my beloved, let us go to the countryside, let us spend the night in the villages. Let us go early to the vineyards to see if the vines have budded, if their blossoms have opened, and if the pomegranates are in bloom—there I will give you my love."

—Song of Solomon 7:10–12

"A Rosebud—God's Design"

When spring comes to us,
Scent of flowers in the air,

A tiny little rosebud,
A flower of God's design.
Perfect in His possession,
Always in His hand,
God unfolds the petals,
The secret's unknown to me,
The tiny little rosebud,
A flower of God's design,
Unfolds with perfection,
The rose in His hand.
As my life lies before me,
With its joy and distress,
He is always near me,
Unfolding all life's petals,
The flower of His design,
Forever in His hand.

"He said that we belonged together because he was born with a flower and I was born with a butterfly and that flowers and butterflies need each other for survival" (Gemma Malley, *The Declaration*).

THE HOUSE OF LOVE

There is a house that sits firmly on a strong foundation. That foundation is love. This love is built, over time and contains the fondest of memories. The first attraction, the first kiss, meeting the families, enjoying a quiet dinner together, touches, smiles, eyes that shine at the sight of the other, birth of the child, special activities and so much more. When things get tough, as they will, this love is where the couple must focus. They must look to the memories and the love foundation that is strong and getting stronger each year. Then there are the bricks and mortar of the house. They are loyalty, commitment, unconditional love, respect, honour, trust, and always being there for each other. If any of the buildings bricks get cracked then, just like in a house structure, the marital relationship weakens. The crack must be repaired and sometimes that is a big job and sometimes not so much. Above this awesome house is a cloud. It represents romantic love. This love comes and goes, just like a cloud. Sometimes it is intense as the rain pours down and sometimes it is just a glow of brilliance as the sun shines through it. Romance must be kept alive between two people or it disappears. Keep the house in great repair, make it the number one priority in life and the people who make up this house will be happy, secure and they will dream together!

When first in a relationship people usually spend as much time together as possible, looking forward to the weekend to be constantly together. After marriage, life responsibilities take over and quality time together may wane. Date nights become extremely important and couples need to focus on this being quality time, not just time together. The phones, job tasks and life in general must be put on hold for the evening that you have dedicated to your spouse. This is time to enjoy each other, just like when you were dating. Dating must never end. As children come into the picture, more time management is needed to have time together. Sometimes this is hard, because if extended family isn't nearby, then babysitters need to be hired. Remember, however, that time together doesn't need to cost money. A walk in the park, window shopping, or other activities together are great. As years go by, you will look back on these memories with joy. So just remember, to make great memories together.

Remember the cloud in the sky, called romantic love? This is the fire that keeps the relationship beautiful. Little heartfelt gifts, preparing a special meal for the other, candlelit times, running a hot bath, a special card, a love note or letter, saying 'I love you' when least expected, snuggling by the fireplace when the kids are in bed—use your imagination.

As a new couple, include your spouse and family as you make your New Year's resolutions. Keep romantic love and spending time together high on the list. Make the Relationship House of Love, your spouse, the priority. Make great memories, love each other with a heart that is overflowing with love, as you enjoy each other.

RELATIONSHIPS THAT LAST

"Going to the Chapel and We're Gonna Get Married" is a popular song that has been recorded by many artists, including the Beach Boys.

Some of the lines say, "And we'll never be lonely anymore. Because we are going to the chapel to get married." It goes on to say, "I'll be his and he'll be mine...until the end of time." The chorus says, "Gee, I really love you and we're gonna get married."

The implication in the song is that if you are lonely, then get married. As well, he will be yours until the end of time and all because of love. So I wonder why there are so many divorces. About 50 percent of first marriages is what I last heard. Couples tell me that they have never been as lonely as they are in their marriage. How sad this is.

This ditty is what we all like to hear. It gives us a good feeling. True enough, marriage can be for life, and it should be because of love, but in reality, as we would expect, there is a whole lot of real life missing in this song.

Relationships need to have elements of maturity to last. Both people in the marriage must be happy and love themselves, and then they can give and add to the other person's happiness and love fully. We cannot make someone else happy, nor can you make them love you.

Love is the foundation of marriage, a place that comes with the commitment to always be with that person. It is where you go to remember the good times and the place where you go to draw strength from when things aren't so good. However, there is a whole lot more to marriage than love. Love just simply is not enough. Each person must be allowed to grow independently, and then they must work hard together to grow in the relationship.

It is always good if we like the other person and they like you! Along with this comes respect, trust, and someone we can tell anything to. Listening skills need to be fully developed, as communication is often what couples tell me is their main problem. Listening and truly hearing from the other person will help allow you to change, grow, make decisions, and make mistakes without feeling judged or criticized. We can then express feelings and emotions freely.

We need to be able to ask for advice and be given good advice. We need to work together to figure out what to do next in difficult situations. Each of us will accept the other person as they are. One can only change oneself.

I have read studies that say that finances, children, and sex are the three top reasons for divorce. We must be prepared. Two healthy mature individuals with great communication skills can handle whatever comes their way, and together they "take the bull by the horns" and love each other anyway. This is what makes a relationship last.

A relationship must be built on a firm, strong foundation. The bricks of the house must never crack, or the foundation will weaken. The foundation is love, and the bricks are things like loyalty, communication, respect, trust, and commitment. In the sky is a bright cloud that is romantic love. This is what keeps the relationship alive and brings infatuation, excitement, and keeps away the boredom. Let's work together and make the relationship last!

CHILDREN

At age twenty-one, I had a miscarriage; I was nine weeks pregnant. I had been in pain and awake all night. My husband had plans for the day, and I was alone and very scared when the miscarriage occurred. I didn't know what to do. I crawled to the kitchen to phone for help. In the hospital, I was lying on the bed, and on the wall was a quote that said, "Do not be afraid. I will never leave you nor forsake you." No one else could see that wall hanging. As I left the room to go home, it disappeared. I knew it wouldn't be allowed in this hospital, as it was a public hospital with no religion attached to it. I believe it was given to me for encouragement at a time when I really needed it. It was two years before I was ready to "try again." Pregnancy wasn't advised, and I was warned that miscarriage was common with diabetic pregnancies. I knew if I miscarried again I wouldn't try a third time. The grief was very real. When finally I became pregnant, I was very happy.

At the first doctor's appointment, abortion was offered. He would send me to a clinic where abortion was legal. I refused. The pregnancy was amazing. The doctor was so sure I would miscarry that I was four months along before he referred me to a gynecologist. I was told that *if* I made it to full term, I would have to have a Cesarean section. Natural childbirth was too dangerous for me and the baby.

I prayed every day for six months to get pregnant, and then I prayed daily for a healthy baby. There are so many stories attached to the pregnancy, but this will suffice for today. In August, my son was born. That is a day I will never forget. My first memory of him was very dark long hair and little round face. He was perfect. As I held him in my arms the next day, I bowed my head and thanked God for this little miracle. A bundle of joy! Above all odds, I had been given a sweet little baby boy—an angel.

We purchased and moved into our home—my palace, I loved that house. What could be more perfect? A house, a husband, a baby, and we even had a puppy.

One day when I was sitting beside my son's hospital bed, I wrote this poem that I later put it to music. The doctor thought he had meningitis. This was later discounted. The doctor didn't give me much hope, as he was very ill. Lots of folks prayed that night, and the next day when I went into the hospital, he was standing up in the crib, reaching for me and laughing. I took him home that day. Awesomeness! I wrote the poem, "My Little Boy."

"My Little Boy"

A young mother one day,
Knelt by her son's bedside
The doctor told her that he would likely die,
The little body was so still lying in that bed
All alone in anguish she prayed.
Jesus, touch this little one,
Yes, He needs your touch just now
Make him well, make him whole
and make him alive,
And Jesus smiled another smile and
He touched my little boy,
He made him well, He made him
whole he made him alive.

And so I thank you today
For that Holy touch from above.
For answering prayer, answering prayer,
Yes, answering my prayer.
And as I watch my little boy play,
Run and shout about today,
I thank you Lord, I praise you Lord,
I need you Lord.
Jesus touch someone today,
Yes, someone needs your touch just now-
Make them well, make them
whole and make them alive
And Jesus will smile another smile
And He will touch your heart and soul
He'll make you well, make you whole
And make you alive.
Thank you, Lord.

"Accept, don't ask, 'Why should this be?' Each happening is a test. For life on earth's a place to learn. The way to live the best" (Chrissy Greenslade).

We purchased our second home in my hometown near where my parents lived—I thought this home would make me happy. We moved in on my son's first birthday.

At age twenty-six in May of that year, a second son was born. My grandfather had passed away in February. A new birth and a final ending, both in the same year.

At six months pregnant, I drove through one of the worst ice storms in Ontario history to get to my gynecologist. I thought he would put me in the hospital, as I was afraid to be miles away from the hospital in this storm, but he sent me home. I drove back home thirty miles—alone.

I was unwell during this pregnancy, and the baby almost died at birth. He was eleven pounds, seven ounces at birth and was in an incubator for several days due to jaundice. A nurse came in and told me that the baby was dying. I called for the pastor and the church and friends to pray. The baby soon stabilized, and a few days later, we left the hospital together.

By now, can you realize why I believe in the power of prayer? God is a good God, and He loves me and you too.

Trials and tribulations came and kept coming, and I just couldn't deal with them; I didn't know what to do. I continued to blame everyone else for my unhappiness. I had lots of issues to deal with and few skills to do that work.

"Charity"

Faith, hope, and charity,
Faith, hope, and charity,
Faith, hope, and charity,
But the greatest of these is
charity.

Sometimes our faith is so strong, yes, so strong,
He moves mountains out of our way,
But Paul tells us we will surely fail,
Without charity, yes, charity is Christ.
We all need hope and have it in Him,
He is our hope every day,
But God's Word tells us that
charity is love,
Yes, charity, charity is love.
We can prophesy, have knowledge, and be so wise,
Help the poor with our wealth,
We can be a martyr and bear our load,
But we need charity, for charity never fails.
So love your neighbour, love your enemy,
Help the despised, and be kind,
Sincere love is felt without a word,
We need love, for charity is love,
Yes,
charity, charity is love.

Just like the chrysalis, I began to change. I drastically changed. I have many times said that if the experiences that follow here hadn't happened and ended in a divorce, that probably something very drastic would have happened to me. I had to get out of the chrysalis that was keeping me bound. I *should* have been happy, but I was unhappy and tried to fill the unhappiness with material things. When that didn't fill the void, I thought it was all about my husband. Some of it was about our relationship, as there was emotional void there; however, he couldn't understand, and neither could I understand what was happening to me. So he was blamed, and I was blamed, and disaster in the name of divorce, took place. With wisdom on my side now, I realize that I should never have been married so young. I needed to grow up before I could be a suitable marriage partner. However, I was married, and as I look back now, who knows what could have happened had I been able at that age to work through my issues because by then, I was carrying a lot of baggage.

Have you ever wondered if your family of origin has a diagnostic mental health diagnosis? Do you think they are antisocial, have multiple personality, or possibly psychopathic? Well, in some cases, that may be true. However, all families are unique with their own dynamics. Some are healthy, and the dynamics are great. Others have problems and are faulty, and others are toxic. However, family is family.

For several years, I didn't have much to do with my family. I had to think of my kids first and work on *me*. I had to remember that I could only change me and that others are responsible for changing themselves if they want to. Each of us has to deal with healing ourselves in our own way. Learning to love yourself, forgiving yourself and others, and having good boundaries are the key. These are processes and take time. A large part of my work is with couples grieving loss, divorce, loss of a child, miscarriage, abortion, and children who have left. Grieving is painful, but just like the pain that comes with birthing a baby, it does get better, and a new life emerges. It does take time.

Chapter Five

DIVORCE

"There is so much good in the worst of us,
And so much bad in the best of us,
That it ill behoves any of us
To find fault with the rest of us!"

—Anonymous

"There's a Hole in My Sidewalk"
By Portia Nelson

Chapter One of My Life. I walk down the street. There's a deep hole in the sidewalk. I fall in. I am lost. I am helpless. It isn't my fault. It still takes forever to find a way out.

Chapter Two. I walk down the same street. There's a deep hole in the sidewalk. I pretend I don't see it. I fall in again. I can't believe I'm in the same place! But it isn't my fault. And it still takes a long time to get out.

Chapter Three. I walk down the same street. There's a deep hole in the sidewalk. I see it there. I still fall in. It's a habit! My eyes are open. I know where I am. It is my fault. I get out immediately.

Chapter Four. I walk down the same street. There's a deep hole in the sidewalk. I walk around it.

Chapter Five. I walk down a different street.

Back then, I found this poem, and it really spoke to my heart. I realized I had been stuck in Chapter Two and for a very long time.

My personal life was out of control! I needed help. I looked for it in relationships with men. Abuse brings pain, and baggage brings more pain. That is exactly what happened. I made many poor choices for the next years, being in and out of relationships, hurting myself, my children, and others. Abuse touched my life over and over again.

I had been to counsellors, and the sexual abuse issues became less important. Counselling helped me put the divorce and the sexual abuse into its proper place. I took the responsibility I needed to and gave the rest away. I was able to get to the place of forgiveness, accepting God's forgiveness, forgiving others and, most of all, myself. I moved on to Chapter Three.

"Peace in the Tumult"

The water ripples over the stones
The horses neigh in the pasture field
The leaves twitter in the breeze
The sun shines through the branches.
Racing, racing, my thoughts race
As the water flows quickly in the brook.
Fish are spawning
My thoughts are breaking
Feelings of rage, confusion, frustration, fear.
Alone again, no one to share
But peace in the tumult
God is peace, He has control,
He knows my need,
He will provide.

"Like a butterfly stuck in a chrysalis, waiting for the perfect moment, I was waiting for the day I could burst forth and fly away and find my home" (Emme Rollins, *Dear Rockstar*).

"Imagine"

A newly developed butterfly
Has just come out of the cocoon
It is sitting on a leaf drying
Its wings, and it must flutter
Until strength comes to it.
Imagine—
It flies close to the leaf, for
Security in its weakness,
Taking time to recover the
Long growth in a safe place.
Waiting, and working, with patience
Imagine—
Strength comes and so for
A time it sits and then it flies
But wait, now there are two
Another butterfly comes, and they
Experience freedom and flying together.
Think about this—
Someone once said, "If love is a choice,
Who would choose such exquisite pain?"
But love is only painful if one chooses not to give it.
Real pain is never experiencing true love.
Experience freedom—love as a butterfly loves.

SEPARATION AND DIVORCE TO NEW BEGINNINGS

I married young, and soon thereafter two children arrived. When they were five and eight years old, their father announced he was going to leave, and there was no turning back. He was the sole financial provider in our home. I was faced with being a single mom with no job and no job availabilities in the small town where we lived. I had to quickly get a plan into place. I chose to go back to school, develop a career, and move to another location. Responsibility—it was all on my shoulders, and now I was alone.

As I work with separating and divorced people, I sometimes reflect back on my personal experience. The definition of divorce in the Webster's dictionary is the "legal dissolution of a marriage by a court..." This reflects the business side of a marriage, and it is difficult; however, there is also the emotional attachment and commitment that are broken and the process of separation. An illustration I use is a ripping apart of a family. It can be compared to a bandage that is ripped from your skin. The ripping apart has a ripple effect from the couple to their children, extended family, and friends. Many people are affected by divorce, and each one reacts. The outcome of a surgery compares to the divorce itself. One is always hoping that the outcome will be favorable.

The stages of grief and loss are experienced many times over and over again. This is different for each situation, as everyone's experience is different. The one that is left usually experiences the most pain at the time of separation. My children said to me, "Mommy, how come when my brother and I fight, we don't get divorced, we become friends again, but you and Daddy are getting a divorce?" It's tough to explain adult decisions to little ones and difficult to look into those little eyes and try to explain.

Finally, when the court process is over and the grieving for dreams lost is finished, life does have a new beginning, new meaning, and new dreams.

"Decisions"

Here I sit in the sunshine contemplating.
Soon a decision will have to be made.
I see the cross-road ahead
Coming closer and closer.
Do I turn, or do I walk on?
I pray for guidance to
Choose the way.
The Bible is my road map,
Jesus said, "I walk with you,
I will guide you
Trust me in the present
For the future when it comes
Will be My will for you
And you will know."
Trust in the Lord with all of your heart and
Lean not unto thine own understanding
In all your ways acknowledge Him
And He shall direct your path.
I weigh it in my wisdom,
Speak to elders who have more
I question and, oh, how I question
The effects on many lives will happen
This is overwhelming to me

Procedure dictates the rules
And so I guess we will see.
So, Lord, guide this process
Bring your will to me
For what can I do without you?
Your will be done now and forever
Let me be your hands, feet, ears, and eyes,
To work as you worked on this earth
With compassion, trust, and gentleness
Lord, reflect these through me, and
The decision will be made.
With praise, love, and thanksgiving.
Amen.

The three years of separation leading up to the divorce were more than difficult. I can't find the words to describe the grieving and the pain I felt. I knew then, and I know now that the marriage had to end, but the pain we instilled on each other and on the children should never have happened. He blamed me, and I blamed him, such immature reactions.

I felt ex-communicated from the church, as all my church positions were taken away from me. I lost my church family, and I felt so judged. I had two friends remaining, and I am grateful for them. They were just there, there was no judgment. I am sure they have no idea how important they were for me just to keep my sanity at that time.

I struggled with Scripture, as I had been taught that divorce is just plain wrong and that it should never happen. Marriage is for life, and I had taken those vows. I searched the Scriptures, and one day I said to the Lord, "If I was to stay in the marriage, I would die. All I can do now is believe that you will forgive me and help me as I continue through this separation and divorce." My thinking became one of openness in decisions regarding divorce. The wall hanging in my hospital room had said, "I will *never* leave you nor forsake you." I placed my trust on that promise. I stood aside and watched as the Lord brought my children to me, and life was restored.

Here is information for those of you who have influence that says that divorce is not good in God's eyes. I believe it is not the best way, but sometimes it is the only way, and God understands that.

If you are contemplating divorce, going through the grieving stages of divorce, or have recently signed those papers, seek the help you need. Lawyers, mediator, financial advisor, real estate expert are some of the professionals to enlist. Psychologically, you have come through a tremendous loss, and even though you think you were prepared for it, there are many stages of grief and loss you will face in the divorce recovery time. Professional counselling can help in this process, as anxiety and depression are present too. One of the questions that clients ask me is, how long will this take? They will say, "I want to get this over as quickly as possible." The answer is, as long as it takes. Lots of things have influence here. How long you were together, usually the more years, the longer it takes to recover. You will have many stages in the divorce recovery. The stages are like an umbrella of denial, mixed emotions, anger, depression, deep sadness, bargaining, the what-if questions you ask yourself, and finally, the letting go and forgiveness stage. Now you don't go through this just one time; the umbrella is the overall grief.

There are many times of grief during the process. Examples are your first trip to the lawyer, seeing him walk away with the children for the weekend, family and friends' questions, and finally receiving the divorce papers—and there are several steps to this one. During all this grief, clients often say my main concern is for my children. I don't want this to affect them, but the truth is it will. They have just lost the family as they have known it from birth. How could it not affect them? So your focus has to go to the children. Children often blame themselves, are very conflicted, feel guilt, maybe ashamed. Depending on their age, it is important to address their questions at their age level. You can't address a five year-old's questions the same as a teenager's. Answer only their questions and do not elaborate. Do not blame the other parent as hard as that may be, even if you believe it is their fault. The children love you both and are struggling to know what to do. Remember, they cannot process this "disaster" in their life because they aren't emotionally mature. They are kids, and they must be allowed to be kids.

One of the most important things is to listen to them. Let them tell you what they need and give it to them if possible. Solicit the help of friends and family; however, they must not take sides, and that is very difficult for family. Do not talk about adult things in front of children or within their earshot. Kids will hear only part of what you say with little understanding and will put their meaning to it, so they will react. Kids show their feelings with behavior. Either they will act out loudly or they will go within and become quiet and probably tell you everything is okay when it isn't. They may try to take care of you, which means they are trying to parent you. This must be discouraged. A child cannot be a confidant. A child must be allowed to be a child through this agonizing time in their life. Remember they are not little adults; they are children. Children have a right to be protected and to have fun! Try very hard to keep them on a schedule, as this will create a sense of security. And lay aside yourself and have fun with your children. Enjoy them. Let them know you will never leave them. You will always be their parent, and you will always love them and be there for them.

Do children come out of this okay? Yes, if their well-being is the focus and if parents can be mature enough themselves to help the children. Counselling is available to help children understand divorce. I had a coworker years ago who told me that she remembered her childhood as being "terrific." Her parents divorced when she was little, and both parents remarried. She said that having two Christmases and two birthdays and four adults who loved her "above and beyond" gave her an awesome childhood.

I include some resources that may help you if you are a Christian and facing divorce. Visit http://

www.hopedivorce.com. Read the book, *Divorce, God's Will?* By Stephen Gola.

You will find the following, "Finally Free," on the Web site for "Hope Divorce." I wish this freeing information had been available when I went through the divorce. The guilt I felt was almost unbearable. Please find your freedom if you are going through devastation and guilt to do with separation and divorce.

- *You* can be *finally free* from the guilt of divorce or from the guilt of being married again after a divorce.
- You NO LONGER have to struggle with the condemnation of guilt from a divorce or being married again. Divorce was never a sin in itself—ever!
- You NO LONGER have to wonder whether the decision to divorce is right or wrong—you will have the knowledge of the truth, and the Holy Spirit Himself will guide you.
- You NO LONGER have to stay single because you have been through a divorce. God wants the guilt to be *fully* cleared from your heart and for you to know what the Scriptures truly have to say about you being married again.
- You NO LONGER have to feel far away from God and feel that He is punishing you because of a divorce or being mar-

ried again. You will find out that your Heavenly Father absolutely loves you and that He has specifically sent this book and Web site to confirm His love to you.

- You NO LONGER have to forfeit your ministry and the calling of God upon your life. God wants you back in His army and to fully carry out and fulfill His will for your life.

- We DO NOT consider divorce as an *option* but only when *necessary*. Most marriage failures are a direct result of selfishness or ignorance on the part of one or both spouses. Nevertheless, we share these truths about divorce and being married again because they are the *truth*.

"There is nothing in a caterpillar that tells you it's going to be a butterfly" (R. Buckminster Fuller).

BANKRUPTCY

At one time, I had to declare bankruptcy. Bankruptcy is a legal proceeding involving a person or business that is unable to repay outstanding debts. I suffered depression and at the same time found myself requiring financial assistance. I could write how dark this time was in my life. The worst part of it all was I was having big problems controlling the diabetes. I do remember the day I went to social assistance and asked for help. I also remember the day I saw a psychiatrist. I remember the first meeting and subsequent meetings with the bankruptcy counsellor. What I can tell you is that these people all were caring and kind to me. It was all I could do to hold it together. Tears were brimming, and my heart felt dead.

With bankruptcy, the financial burden was lifted, and I started to be able to think of what I needed to do next. The psychiatrist was amazing, and usually he just let me talk, and he answered my questions. I don't remember how long I saw him, probably six months, and God bless him, he retired. He was very nonjudgmental, and he encouraged me. I spent hours outside walking and climbing and sitting near the water. Water has always been a healing place for me. The sound of the waves and the beauty of its color and the fish that swam nearby—all were a part of my healing. I walked and talked with God. I was so alone, but I really wasn't alone at all.

My father, who was formally uneducated but a great businessman, knew something was wrong, and he asked me what was going on. I told him I had financial issues that I didn't know how to get out of. He helped me with the payment I had to make just to claim bankruptcy. I didn't share this financial crisis with many folks, but those I did were supportive. However, I know from others this isn't always the case. Bankruptcy often brings with it great shame. It took six years to get my name cleared and to start building my credit rating. The steps through bankruptcy weren't hard because I took the attitude that each step is a little closer to getting me back on my feet. I regained my health. I got a job. Then I walked into a bank to cash my first paycheck and was told I had to have a bank account to do so. When I explained that I had bankruptcy but that I needed to cash my paycheck, the teller just shook her head. I then asked to speak to the manager. When she heard my story, she said, "I have a Christmas gift for you today," and she opened a bank account for me. For anyone reading this, if you have financial problems, consider all other options first, as I did, but I can tell you there is life after bankruptcy. It was many years ago for me. It is history!

Chapter Six

CAREER

"It's never wise to analyze, the future with a kind
Of gloomy trait to calculate, the
troubles we may find.
Whatever may occur each day, in
life's demanding school,
The future's fine, if we outline—let optimism rule."

—J.M. Robertson

Walt E. Disney said, "If you dream it, you can do it. Always remember that. This whole thing was started with a dream and a mouse."

I had a dream. My dream was to be the best counsellor I could be. My education and career unfolded. I was determined, and I persevered.

At age thirty-four, I graduated with a Bachelor of Science degree in Nutrition. This training was in wholistic health nutrition and was back in the day when the health craze was just beginning. I was interested in nutrition because of my own health issues with diabetes but more so because I had two little boys who suffered with allergies, asthma, and symptoms such as hyperactivity. I found out what books were needed for the course, purchased and read them, and then after the divorce, I was all ready to do the coursework and exams. I was trained and prepared to do nutrition counselling. However, as one person said to me, I was ten years ahead of my time, and I found I couldn't support my children this way. It then became a hobby. However, I had learned basic counselling strategies and techniques too, which furthered my education in the counselling field.

While working in management, I obtained a diploma in Business Management, a General Social Work certificate, and a General Sexual Abuse certificate. Moving to British Columbia, I went on to achieve a Master of Ministry in Christian Counselling and a Doctorate of Philosophy in Christian Counselling. These were obtained by long-distance education and in-person attendance, all while working full time and raising children as a single mom. I graduated in 1998 with the Ph.D. Walking across the stage, I declared, "I have achieved, and I have won. I am a woman of perseverance." I didn't have a student loan, and I completed my education debt-free. This was my dream. I made life happen through hard work and perseverance.

Education didn't stop there, as I am a sponge for learning. I am an avid reader, and I have taken hundreds of educational seminars, workshops, and conferences. I listen to motivational speakers, but my clients are my best teachers. I learn so much from their stories and from them. Sharing is a beautiful thing.

I empathize with working mothers. My heart was at home with my children. I wanted to be there for them evenings and weekends. I wanted to do all the mommy things and attend all the school functions. However, the reality of being a single mom meant that I could do some things and not others. I had to choose and prioritize. Working out of the home was a necessity, and because I was uneducated, so was the education path I chose. I was fortunate enough to choose the field and industry that I absolutely loved, and I flourished and enjoyed the training and set my sights on being the very best counsellor I could be. I chose non-traditional education because I made the decision that every education subject I would take would benefit me directly in my work. I looked at traditional education studies, and, even though I knew I would make more money, I chose mostly non-traditional education that fit with my belief system and with the not for profit industry. However, my education and experience did eventually take me to the corporate world. So a little history—I started my career in Ontario, Canada, in door-to-door sales. I became top salesperson, in Canada, with two companies. I went on to become a women shelter counsellor and later executive director. Still in Ontario, I took the position of executive director of a justice initiatives organization. I then moved west to Edmonton, Alberta, and became executive director of a family resource center. My next move was to the amazing province of British Columbia and one of my dream jobs, being a coordinator of a sexual abuse program. Later, I opened a private practice, and for thirteen years, I did private work. When I entered the corporate world, the job took me back to Edmonton, Alberta, and I was a telephone counsellor, then a regional manager, finally a frontline counsellor, and lastly where I am today in private clinical practice in Edmonton, Alberta.

If you were to ask me which position I liked the best, I couldn't tell you because each one opened new doors and taught me so much. Each one was my dream job. When I was starting my social work education at the University of Waterloo in Kitchener, Ontario, I had one lecturer who impressed me to continue on the path of education I was pursuing. I remember her career story and how she said that social work had opened so many fascinating avenues of work for her. Now, today, I sit here writing my story, and I can say the same thing.

I have another awesome memory of someone I admired and wanted to fashion my career after. She was a counsellor in Brantford, Ontario. I had connections with her when I was executive director of the women's shelter, and so when I needed counselling for myself and my son, I contacted her. I remember one day, while I was waiting for my son to join me after his session with her, I was in the waiting room. On the wall was a certificate of her achieving her master's degree. I stood and stared at that certificate and said to myself, "One day, I will achieve a certificate like this too." I had no idea how I could possibly do that, as I saw no way clear to go back to school; however, shortly thereafter, I started my university courses, graduated to seminary, and when I reached the master level, I remembered that day. I am so thankful that counsellor gave me a dream. When I got to the master level, I then had to decide if I wanted to continue and complete a Ph.D. It took me a year of contemplation, and I decided to do so. One of the reasons was I wanted to do a Ph.D. thesis. Most folks would tell me I was crazy to want to do such a thing, as it is no easy feat, but I wanted to put together much work that I had done, and my thesis was born, "Historic Female Childhood Sexual Abuse," from a Christian counsellor's perspective. This was therapy for me, and I had to reach into the innermost part of my being, as it was my own story researched, relived, and written. I walked across that stage to receive my document, humbled and strengthened. Nobody had to be proud of me; I had lived it and accomplished great things in the name of the Father, the Son, and the Holy Spirit, and through His name may all be glorified. With a lot of hard work and determination, I accomplished my education goal, and along with it great healing.

Burnout. There have been several times in my career when I have burned out. Wikipedia says, "Burnout is a type of psychological stress. Occupational burnout or job burnout is characterized by exhaustion, lack of enthusiasm and motivation, feelings of ineffectiveness, and also may have a dimension of frustration or cynicism, and as a result reduced efficacy within the workplace. Occupational burnout is typically and particularly found within human service professions. Professions with high levels of burnout include social workers…"

Compassionate burnout was just starting to be talked about when I was executive director of the women's shelter. I hadn't heard of such a thing until then. I am, by nature, a counsellor and encourager. I remember as a child I was the one who befriended the children who had no friends. I felt badly for people who were being mistreated. I was a very sensitive child. Because of my personality and sensitivity, I gave and I gave and I gave. I didn't realize at that time that I am also more introverted and that extroverted exercises are more difficult for me. I also had no idea that I needed recovery time or what that looked like. These things I had to learn. At that time, I picked up stray cats and people alike. I took on their burdens and felt so deeply sorry for them. Now with some maturity and understanding, I can trace back through my life how this was awesome and amazing but also destructive to myself. People loved me because I gave and I gave and I gave. I had no idea how to care for myself and monitor my deep caring.

No one can give all the time and not take care of themselves. This leads to burnout, which it did.

Women's shelter work is stressful due to the nature of the work. On top of that, I was executive director of a new shelter, and I was without any management experience, so I made a lot of mistakes, and I was on a fast learning curve. I had entered a world totally unknown to me, and I didn't know how to establish my boundaries for self-preservation. I was in the position over four years, and the hardest part of all the learning was when staff turned on me as their leader. Consequently, there was lots of staff turnover. Eventually, trying to be everything to all people, the board of directors, the staff, the community, and the clients, I burned out and realized I needed to make a big change in my life.

With this realization, I knew I would have to leave the community and that would disrupt my children. They didn't take to the move well at all. An organization in Kitchener, Ontario, contacted me and offered me a job of executive director with them. I accepted and saw this as a step to a greater move, as I had also decided I wanted to leave my familiar home ground and move west.

The next burnout I experienced was when I received the letter of estrangement from my sons. This time, the burnout was primarily caused by personal issues. My relationship was ending, my children had chosen to stay in Edmonton rather than come with me to British Columbia, the new job that I took, my dream job, did not work out well. I left with heartbreak and burnout again. Too much negativity in my personal and professional world seemed to break me. Change had to happen again. I felt very alone. I started the journey of looking closely at what I needed to change in myself to continue in life and get back on my feet. I took two months away from the job, at which time I decided to leave and do private work and work on my own issues. Burnout is not a fun thing. It is depression mixed with anxiety and extreme fatigue.

This is when I decided to seek a way to complete my master's degree. I learned to better monitor myself as a diabetic and to put appropriate boundaries in place so I was emotionally protected. I haven't suffered burnout again since then, even in very difficult times. However, depression has affected me and is sometimes a part of living with diabetes.

Chapter Seven

FRIENDSHIP

"The butterfly is a flying flower,
The flower a tethered butterfly."
—Ponce Denis Ecouchard Lebrun

"My Best Friend is Jesus"

Jesus is the giver of life in troubled times,
He shows me the way that I must go,
He's always there to help me if I only ask,
He's the best friend I could ever have.
He's the best friend,
I could ever have.
There are times in this old earth
When He seems far away,
I know this is me and
I must go to Him

He's not so far away
If I only ask
He's the best friend
I could ever have.
At times when I can't even find the words to say,
He sends a friend to help me on my way,
Each time I need a helping hand He sends someone,
To show me He's my friend and He's my stay.
So be a friend to someone
Who needs you today
Let Christ shine through your life to them
They need your love from
Christ above, whatever their state
Just love them and
Show them He is their friend.
Just love them and
Show them He is their friend.

MY FRIEND—JOSEPH

Our friendship was only seven weeks long. I lost him to death when we were both thirty-seven years old. We both were Type 1 diabetics, and we both were diagnosed at age seven. We met when I was hospitalized to change my insulin from one kind to another. He was a wonderful friend, and the common understanding of living with a chronic illness drew us close. It was as if we had known each other our whole life. He was handsome and well-spoken. He talked to me about the fact that he had been told he wouldn't have much time left on this earth. He was suffering the complications of diabetes. He was a heavy drinker and smoker. His job had taken him to many dinners where alcohol was a part of work. We talked about life in general, but mostly we joked and laughed and cried together. I shared my Christian experiences with him, and he accepted the Lord into His heart with me in the hospital that day. I was with him when he passed away, and I was able to make sure he was well taken care of and I could say good-bye. When I said to him one day in passing, "What will I ever do without you?" he replied, "I don't have that answer, but I know you are a strong woman, and you will be okay. Just get a good education and live life to its fullest because the cure for diabetes is on its way, and you will be here to experience it." I have surpassed his life in this world by thirty years at the time of this writing. The cure is still on its way!

Tuesday was our day. We met on a Tuesday, he died on a Tuesday, and he called me every morning on Tuesday. Never did a Tuesday go by without me hearing from him. In fact, I heard from him every Tuesday for seven weeks. It is one of my most cherished memories. My friend, I will always remember your smile.

MY TRAVELLER FRIEND—JEREMY

I had a river behind my apartment, and I wrote poetry there. My traveller friend was travelling abroad. His safety was always on my mind.

"My Walk along the River"

I walked and talked with you today
The sun shone bright and the mountains spoke clear
The snow on the tops glistened as I watched, but
The river ran cold.
Thinking of you in a faraway land
Knowing it is hot and humid and so different there
Wondering if you too are looking at the calendar
Does the river run cold?
My heart is happy but it is also sad
I walked and talked with you today
The joy in my heart is scared that
The river will run cold.
Is your heart happy, or is it sad too?
How are you remembering me, or are you?
Do you have joy in your heart that fears
The river will run cold?
My only wish for you is
Peace, hope, and love
And the greatest of these is
love.

"Friendship"

I sit and wonder and wait for
You, my friend.
Feeling compassion and excitement for
You, my friend.
You are a wonderful person
With an adventuresome spirit,

I sit and wonder and wait.
Amazed—I dream
I wonder and wait,
Where are you my friend, where are you?
Do you hear me, do you feel my prayers?
My eyes want to see deep into your spirit,
Please, come to me.
Come and bring your spirit
As only you can do.
So, where are you?
When will I know?
What will you say?
How will you be?
I want to hear the stories
The wonder of it all, because
I know Cambodia has changed your life,
Forever.
This story was told to me and—
"I Love You"

I met a fifty-six-year-old Persian man
We had many wonderful hours of talking together
On going our separate ways,
He parted by saying, "I love you."
Strangers but one in spirit and in truth
Sharing words of kindness one heart, together
Lives so different but one in spirit
I will always remember, "I love you."

MY HIGH SCHOOL FRIEND TODAY AND FOREVER—CHERYL

"One should keep old roads and old
friends" (German Proverb).

Leaving the little one-room school with around eighteen classmates to enter a huge school of some one hundred children was terrifying to me. I had seldom been away from my family and never on a bus. I didn't know Getting up early and riding the bus with the kids was excruciatingly painful and tough for me. Worse of it all was that most of those kids knew each other, but they didn't know me. Then at the school, a huge school, my greatest fear was getting lost and being embarrassed. The first time I saw and met my friend, we were in the school cafeteria. I remember saying to her, "Will you be my friend?" and she agreed. How relieved was I, I had a friend. Both being introverted, we didn't have much to do with others at school except the classroom interaction. We often slept over at each other's house. Riding that dreadful bus was made easier when doing it with a friend.

After high school, she went her way and I mine. She became a nurse, and I became a mother. We soon lost our close connection, seeing each other infrequently. But eighteen years ago now, I so needed her, my friend, and we have talked often since then. We can talk about the past, present, and future. We have it all covered. Lots of healing has been accomplished just through our talks. It is awesome having a friend that, even though we live miles apart and at times didn't talk for months or even years at a time, when we do talk it is as if no time has lapsed. We have stood by each other, supporting and helping each other. She has listened to my stories, and I have listened to hers. There is love with no judgment. Now we are older and we both have disabilities that are a challenge, life is different but ever the same with us. We are very close, I don't think sisters could be any closer.

"To My Soroptimist Club and
Female Friends Everywhere"

I have found friends, friends who care,
They live the whole world over.
Women who love life,
Women who are strong,
Women who help women,
Empower, empower, empower.
As a young woman, I needed
Help, encouragement and to be empowered.
I was struggling as a single mom
Working full-time and, oh, so tired
With two children by the hand—when
The Soroptimist Training Award
Chosen, I was chosen, it was mine.
The next semester courses were paid for
With the help I received, no longer did I worry for
I completed my diploma and onward to my goal!
Working hard in social service agencies

THE BUTTERFLY FLIES

Helping others as I could
Finally, the day arrived when a Ph.D. was mine.
Thirteen years in private family counselling
Children grown and doing well
I returned to the place where it all started
To Soroptimists and I must tell—
The story of my award and the life it brought to me
Through kind and loving women
Who care when it seems there is no sign.
I am excited with each step
As I learn and go forward
Women teaching women and
Women helping women
It is my time to give
My time to empower women with
An organization I believe in.
To take on the challenges of life
Domestic violence and trafficking
So demoralizing to women and their children
Public education, important as it is
Educate all who will listen to the
stats and stories told.
We all know of the hardships women endure
So, give, empower, teach, and train.
Women helping women—
Soroptimists, Soroptimists, Hurray for Soroptimists!

Chapter Eight

ABUSE ISSUES

"It has been said that something as small as
the flutter of a butterfly's wing can ultimately
cause a typhoon halfway around the world."

—Author unknown

BULLYING

For a moment, I want to point you to a research
report called 'Voices from the Edge'. Researched by
Route One Resource Services and Alison Whitley,
November 2016—January, 2017. You may wonder
why I put it in the domestic violence chapter. Well,
abuse is abuse and kids act out behaviours they have
learned, and so do adults. These behaviours must
be challenged and changed. The following article,

which is some of my story of personal bullying, is in the 'Voices from the Edge' report.

EVA'S STORY OF BULLYING

Eva was bullied in public school decades ago, before bullying was understood like it is today. There was a bully in her school who would tease, chase, and scare the younger students. He would lead other boys to do similar things. He was about three years older than Eva.

She was a Type 1 diabetic child, and having to go to the bathroom was a common occurrence and made her stand out. One day, when the teacher had left the school for an hour, the bully chased her into the bathroom and wouldn't allow her to use it unless she used it with him present, adding that he wouldn't leave. She refused and told him to leave her alone. He didn't touch her, but she was afraid of what might happen. She told no one. This kind of abuse was reported daily in their school, and not just with her.

The bully would even undermine the teacher so he could bully the kids on the playground. He seemed to know where the teacher was and he would go behind her back and do things that she would never find out about. Eva said that if he hadn't been there, the school might have been a nice place to be.

In light of her experience over the years, she now thinks about how she never told anybody. She will never know what may have happened if she had. No help was available for either the abuser or victims in their small community. From what she hears, the guy is still a bully today—and he is in his sixties now.

Eva has felt the impact left over from bullying, over the years. When she thinks back, she can still feel that fear of being threatened and alone. No one else would come near him—everyone was afraid of him.

One outcome is that it influenced her career. Her first job was as a social worker for battered/abused women. She now works with youth and marriage/divorce counselling. She helps kids build their self-esteem so they feel better about themselves. Bullying can pull people down. She always advises that kids go to their parents (if they can) and talk with them about issues and figure them out. Even so, kids are still afraid to talk—the parents go to the school, and the bully is still there. Eva thinks that things are still not working but doesn't have the answer.

Eva doesn't know what was going on in the bully's childhood home. Even as an adult senior, she has been told that he is still a bully. He's a farmer, and other farmers are concerned. He's very arrogant. He was at her family farm sale, which was a difficult time for her, and he was saying things against her father. Her father tells her that the bully has treated other men, families, etc., badly.

Let's do all we can to put an end to bullying. It affects children's lives, and it happens on playgrounds, when kids leave the school for home, in the workplace, and in the home.

"Husbands love your wives, just as Christ also loved the church and gave himself up for her."

—Ephesians 5:25

My story continues:

Entering into the arena of domestic violence. The studying and meeting battered and abused women made me examine my own experiences. I knew I had to confront one of my abusers, and I did so. If you decide to do the same, make sure you are not alone and that you do it in a protected place such as a public space. This is for your safety. I had police on backup call and others nearby. It was most difficult because he wouldn't take any responsibility. It was the day I decided to forgive not for his sake but for mine. I needed to be released from this thing, and it started to happen that day. I had hoped for healing, and I knew this was the only way it could take place. Years later, I am still happy that day happened. It had to.

In intimate relationships, I experienced being punched in the face, verbal attacks against my personality and beliefs, sarcasm, control of money, interrupting my sleep, control of food, isolation from friends, destroying and taking my prized possessions, threat with a weapon, and perceived threats. Why do women and why did I remain in these relationships? Societal beliefs, Christian beliefs, community responses, background of abuse, learned behavior, fear of being alone, finances, education level, expectations of others, children, psychological brain-washing—this is a list of reasons. I am not going to go into any detail because my story is very typical of the thousands of women, who enter into abusive relationships.

I had to learn to trust. Trust was very difficult for me. Anxiety has been with me all my life. I have experienced it and sometimes still do. I remember the panic attacks and my heart pounding so hard it was about to jump out of my chest. I did eventually come to the place of realizing that not all people will hurt me. I wrote this poem during one of those times.

"Trust"

There are many times in life as I wonder,
And I feel God's protection ever near,
I will never forget the times He has warned me,
So gently, never alarming, He is love.

Satan wants me to be afraid, He wants me to fear,
Ever human, I've made mistakes and I do fear,
Then the tender loving master says, "I love you,"
Lean on Me, have no fear, I am love.

Then He gently, oh, so gently surrounds me,
With compassion, I feel His perfect peace,
In my small and fragile state, He is with me,
I am strong, I have no fear, He is love.

There is a difference now in my life,
Jesus fills me with His love and abiding peace,
I want to stay close by his side and never fear,
Never fear, never fear, for God is love.

I know Jesus will always be there,
I love Him so, oh how I need Him in my life,
He enriches and fulfills my every need,
Remember, Jesus is the conqueror over fear.

I always picture myself when I get into a situation that I am like a bull with horns, and I just put my head down, and I go through, and all must get out of my way. I will succeed, I am strong, and I deserve freedom.

There is help.

If you are suffering from domestic violence where you are being humiliated, not allowed to have your own opinion, being yelled at or ignored, threatened that if you leave he will take your children, psychologically abused—with reference to weapons—hit, beaten, or experiencing items being broken in your home on purpose, then please pay special attention to what I am entering here.

Abuse is staggering. It is destructive of person and of that person's spirit. There is emotional abuse, psychological abuse, sexual abuse, and physical abuse. Women who have been beaten have told me how the emotional abuse bruises the heart and takes a very long time to heal. In comparison, a beating that can easily kill causes bruises that heal relatively quickly. The cycle of violence is made up of three parts: the violent event, the honeymoon phase, and the buildup of tension. The cycle keeps repeating. Women will get to the place where they know when the tension is building leading to an event, and they will sometimes do something to trigger the event just to get it over with so he will become sorry, bring flowers, and be lovingly affectionate again.

> "YOUR ABUSIVE PARTNER DOESN'T HAVE A PROBLEM WITH HIS ANGER; HE HAS A PROBLEM WITH YOUR ANGER.
>
> One of the basic human rights he takes away from you is the right to be angry with him. No matter how badly he treats you, he believes that your voice shouldn't rise and your blood shouldn't boil. The privilege of rage is reserved for him alone. When your anger does jump out of you—as will happen to any abused woman from time to time—he is likely to try to jam it back down your throat as quickly as he can. Then he uses your anger against you to prove what an irrational person you are. Abuse can make you feel straitjacketed. You may develop physical or emotional reactions to swallowing your anger, such as depression, nightmares, emotional numbing, or eating and sleeping problems, which your partner may use as an excuse to

belittle you further or make you feel crazy."

—Lundy Bancroft, *Why Does He Do That?: Inside the Minds of Angry and Controlling Men*

"An abuser can seem emotionally needy. You can get caught in a trap of catering to him, trying to fill a bottomless pit. But he's not so much needy as entitled, so no matter how much you give him, it will never be enough. He will just keep coming up with more demands because he believes his needs are your responsibility, until you feel drained down to nothing."

—Lundy Bancroft, *Why Does He Do That?: Inside the Minds of Angry and Controlling Men*

What can you do if you are in an abusive relationship?

You *must* have a safety plan, a backup plan that you can put in place quickly when needed. Make sure you have phone numbers in a safe place that you can access quickly and where he can't find them.

Have a safety plan.

When there is abusive behavior in your home, for your safety, it may be necessary for you to leave. If there is a chance this may happen, you must have a safety plan. It can be a big help, as it is difficult to think things through when emotionally upset. It will assist you in your efforts to leave. If a violent incident is happening, move yourself to an area that has an exit to the outdoors. It may be necessary for you to run to a neighbor for help or to get them to call the police. Get away from the kitchen and away from any weapons. Have people who have consented and are willing to assist you with money or a place to stay.

Below are instructions about what to do after getting a Protective Order (such as having copies made) and what to do in the event of a violation of the Protective Order as well as a list of what to take when you leave (i.e., money, keys, medication) and emergency numbers (police, prosecuting attorney, and women's shelter):

1. Call the police.
2. Call a shelter.
3. Get counselling.
4. Inform friends and family if it is safe to do so.
5. Open your own bank account or hide money for emergency use.
6. Take important papers with you, such as your marriage license, birth certificate for yourself and your children, etc.

Go to http://www.domestic violence.com for more information and to find resources in your area.

A WOMAN SPEAKS

My experience leaving my husband of forty-three years was probably the most difficult decision I ever made. The Christian community does not always support this type of action. I was feeling judged and I needed to find someone to talk with that could help me through the feelings of guilt. If there were bruises on my body maybe people would understand, but my bruises were on my emotions and my spirit. I prayed that God would provide a Christian counsellor who would show me empathy and aide me in my healing. God led me to Eva Shaw and as I met with her for counselling and told my story, I was able to hear the gentle tones of understanding as she encouraged me to answer some of my own questions. She listened intently without passing judgement on me and for that I am very grateful. I would leave the sessions with homework reading to do and questions to direct at myself to get a better understanding of what I had been feeling for years and why I actually found the courage to leave this lifelong relationship.

I had never admitted to myself before that I was living with an abusive spouse. The counsellor didn't tell me that, she gave me material to read from the internet and books on relationships. Through the ministry of my counsellor I was able to identify the type of relationship my husband and I had. Sad to say it was very unhealthy and I needed to do a lot of work on myself because there were a lot of damaged emotions that had been buried and needed to be felt and dealt with in a healthy manner. Through a lot of reading, talking, and introspection and prayer I was able to uncover a lot of truths. John's gospel states that you shall know the truth and the truth will set you free. I was now able to identify a lot about both my husband's and my personality. I knew that I needed to set up healthy boundaries and that I could never go back and live the way I had been living.

Some people might say, "Why didn't you speak up more, or louder and say what you were feeling about the control issues and the anger?" I did but it only escalated his anger and my fear. So, "why didn't you leave years ago?" For the longest time I was afraid to leave, but it reached a point where I was afraid to stay." My counsellor assisted in educating me about relationships and self-discovery and when I had made my final decision that I wasn't going back she informed me of a divorce symposium that was taking place where I could receive direction from lawyers on how to go about legal separation and divorce. There were also all types of professionals at the symposium to assist a person in their journey to personal independence and emotional, financial, and physical avenues of healing. I am thankful for the ministry of, "Make Life Happen" and I will pray that others will find this open door of liberation and find their wings to fly.

Chapter Nine

ESTRANGED FROM
A CHILD

"Love is like a butterfly, beautiful and delicate…
If you truly care for it, you'll do whatever you can
to make it happy, even if that means letting it go."

—Scott Pemberton

There's no greater loss in the whole world than being estranged from a child. I have heard this from many clients and have experienced this loss myself.

One day I wrote:

Estranged from my child
Worse than most loss I can imagine.
Estrangement from a child.

You birth a baby
You care so deeply
Rocking him to sleep every night
Holding him when he cries
Pictures of the first day of school
Saving to give this child a guitar
and lessons for years to come.

Providing a new house and room
for friends and music
Providing transportation whenever you needed it
Trying to teach the basics to pre-
pare you for the future
Grocery buying, food preparation, buy-
ing clothes, budgeting money.
Begging him not to go…you are too young, but…
He was determined…

Then I received the ultimate pain of my life
A letter of divorcement cutting me
off from being your mother.
I am your mother, I will always be your mother
That cannot change.

I did things wrong. I had no expe-
rience of being a mom.
I was emotionally hurting, and my pain was so deep.
Years of dealing with my own life
where I had little to give
He grew to hate me and then despise me.

THE BUTTERFLY FLIES

Years later, I met him with others present.
He greeted me by my name
It was pleasant
Our talk, I thought, was a
start to healing, but…
then nothing, and I was forced to give up.

He is a grown man now with choices all his own
I wish things were different
I wish we could heal together
But I had to let him go,
No use in trying any longer.

He is a successful businessman.
With a family of his own
He has done well in life, but I won-
der, does he ever miss his mom?
I used to think when my boys were small
We will always look after each other. But not so…

I have the most precious memories.
Baby in my tummy kicking,
Baby at birth and how amazing he was,
The first smile, his first haircut, his first picture,
His first crawling and then the first step,
His childhood sweetheart, and the prom,
The amazing music that he
played, sang, and created.

Awesome memories forever
No one can take them from me.

I miss you my son.
I wish you all the best.

If you are estranged from a child,
I know your heart
I feel the pain
I know the remorse
I know the anger
I wish for you to
Live your life and be free!
There is no other choice.

The first thing I want to say to you if you have experienced estrangement from a child is that it is *not* your fault. It took me a very long to time to accept that it wasn't my fault. I did the very best I could do with what I had to work with. Our actions as a parent or our lack of action did not cause this. It is a response to anxiety, co-dependency, and lack of boundaries as well as disrespect to the parents. Shutting down and running away are what people do when they don't know a better way. The ability to solve differences is not there. The person who has cut off contact doesn't know how to address and resolve the problem. They think that discontinuing communication will resolve the problem; however, nothing is resolved.

If you have this issue in your family, please visit http://www.empoweringparents.com. Here are some steps to follow that I have taken from their Web site. I quote:

If you're in this difficult position, here are five things you can do:

1. *Don't go at this alone. Get support.* Being cut off by your child, with no ability to understand, communicate, and resolve things, is difficult enough. That's why being connected to others who love and understand you is particularly important. In addition to reaching out to friends and family, consider joining a support group. If you are not able to function at your best, get some professional help.

2. *Don't cut off in response.* You are not the one cutting ties; your child is. Don't cut off your child in response. Continue to reach out to him, letting him know that you love him and that you want to mend whatever has broken. Send birthday and holiday messages as well as occasional brief notes or e-mails. Simply say that you are thinking about him and hope to have the opportunity to reconnect. Send your warmth, love, and compassion—as you get on with your life.

3. *Step back, look, and don't feed the anger.* It's understandable to feel angry. And in their attempt to be supportive, friends and family may fuel your feelings of betrayal, inadvertently increasing your anger. Anger is natural but not helpful. Step back and try

to understand what led to this estrangement. What patterns were operating in your family dance? If you can look at your family from a more factual vantage point, it may feel less personal. No one is to blame. Now if the door opens, you will be in a much better position to reconcile.

4. *If the door opens, listen to your child without defending yourself.* Listen with an open heart. Listen to her perceptions of what wrongs took place. Even if you disagree with her, look for the grains of truth. Be willing to look at yourself. It's hard to hear these criticisms, especially if your intentions were misunderstood. So prepare yourself to handle this. Your adult child may need to hold onto blame as a way to manage her own anxiety. Just letting her know that you hear her will go a long way. Keep in mind that she too had to be in tremendous pain to reach the point of shutting you out. Try to empathize with her pain rather than get caught up in the hurt and anger.

5. *Focus on yourself, not your child.* If you do begin communicating again, you will be in a position to learn from the mistakes of the past and work toward an improved relationship. Put your efforts into changing yourself, not your child. Let go of your resentments regarding the estrangement.

Understand his need to flee…and forgive him. Get to know the adult child you have, not the child you think he should have been. Allow him to get to know you. If your child still has made no contact, grieve the loss and know there is still hope. Try to manage your anxiety and do the right thing by staying in touch with him in a non-intrusive way: occasionally and lovingly. Things may change. Rather than blame yourself or your child for this pain, use your energy to learn about yourself and your own family history and patterns in your other relationships. Look for other patterns of cutting off in your family tree.

Your pain is real. Be mindful and compassionate of it, but don't allow it to define or overwhelm you. Put the focus on what you have control of: your own life.

Chapter Ten

MY CHRISTIAN TESTIMONY

"Butterflies are self-propelled flowers."

—R.H. Heinlein

What is my testimony? It is my story of my creator's love for me. As a professional and Christian counsellor, I say to you there is hope, there is freedom.

I am a Christian. This is my choice. I was not born with the decision already made. I had to choose. For Jesus said in John 14:6, "I am the way, the truth, and the life, and no one comes to the father [God] but by me." And John 3:16 says, "For God so loved the world that He gave His only son, that whosoever believed in Him would not perish but have everlasting life."

My story includes how I came through difficult times and how my faith was built in Him. He is a faithful God. Christianity isn't about having an easy life; it is about having Jesus walk beside you as a friend. When there is no one else, there is God the Father, Jesus the Son, and the Holy Spirit who speaks to our heart.

A LITTLE GIRL'S HEART

Have you ever sat and studied a child? Have you really listened and watched an innocent little one, a gift to the world? What wonderment! A child has big eyes to take in every sight. A child asks many questions until satisfied with the answer and then soon asks more. A child laughs when happy and cries when hurt. Is it a surprise that Jesus welcomed the children to sit on His knee? Jesus loved the children. He told us to be like the little children with an accepting nature and uncomplicated faith.

I once knew a little girl who lived on a farm. She was fascinated with the animals, the pond where she skated, and the vegetable garden where she helped her grandmother plant and weed. The baby chicks were fun. Her inquisitiveness brought questions about Noah's ark. "Just how did he care for two of every animal of the world?"

Her grandmother believed that Jesus Christ is the Savior of the world, and soon the child was asking questions. Every day, for years, Grandma told the child Bible stories. As she grew older, Grandma told of her experience of salvation at a mission, near where she worked as a young woman and where she accepted Jesus as her personal savior. The elderly woman told the child of Jesus's love and how she had been physically healed. Prayer became significant, and the little girl would rhyme a bedtime prayer and later grew to pray from her heart and soul.

She was a beautiful child with long blonde ringlets, a captivating smile and eyes that were the window to her soul. You see, she had attended Sunday school and soon asked Jesus into her heart. Joy poured into her soul and overflowed into her music and songs. Folks enjoyed as she sang and played at street corner meetings, church, school, and wherever she was asked.

The little girl and the neighborhood farm children attended a one-room country school. She was very excited about her newfound friend, Jesus, and she wanted to share her joy with friends and family. She asked her school playmates if they would like to meet with her at recess and learn about Jesus.

She wondered, *How do I do this?* After praying and talking to trusted adults, she put together a short program and shared it daily with the children. Bible readings, stories, prayers, songs, and love were combined to keep the children interested in the reason their friend, the little girl, was filled with joy. Diligently she shared, hoping her friends would love Jesus just like her.

As time passed and the children grew older, they were off to different schools and later college, marriage, and careers. The now grown-up little girl often wondered if anyone really understood how much she loved Jesus. She wondered if anyone had accepted Him into their heart in those tender years. However, she also had moved far away and fell out of touch with her school friends.

One day, as an adult, the little girl returned to her hometown. The phone rang, and a familiar voice from long ago asked if they could have lunch together. Sitting in a bistro with lunch before them, the longtime friend began to softly cry.

She recently suffered the death of both parents. The woman continued to say that she arranged the meeting to thank her for sharing about Jesus at the little country school house at recess. Do you remember?

With her long blond hair falling over her shoulders, the adult little girl whispered, "Yes, I remember." The woman went on and, with much emotion, said, "I had never heard of Jesus's love. I didn't know He loved me. You see, your joy brought Jesus to me. Your sharing made a big difference in my life."

We sometimes hear the cliché, "out of the mouth of babes." How true it is. A little girl's heart and the joy within changed the life of another precious child. When we see a child, take time to stop, look, and listen to the wisdom coming from the child's heart. Let's be diligent to teach our children God's love. Always remember "a little girl's heart."

"My Decision and Journey as a Christian"

As I walked down life's pathway all alone
I met a friend called Jesus on the way
I asked Him to come into my heart and live within
And I would love Him, yes, love Him forevermore.
The path was narrow, the path was
straight, the path to home
He was guiding me on the rough uneven road
I was trusting, ever trusting in my Lord
As I walked down life's pathway I wasn't alone.
The way is sometimes weary
And the way is sometimes hard
The way is always exciting
Because I am trusting in His way
As I let Him lead me on
Ever trusting, ever loving
He's leading me home.
One day He said to my heart, "You
need to walk on in My way
Will you serve me, will you trust me forevermore?"
Then He said, "I will lead and not just guide
Step by step ever trust me, I must lead."
The way was sometimes weary, and
The way was sometimes hard
The way was always exciting
Because I was trusting in His word.
The way was His way
As I let Him guide me on
Ever trusting, ever loving
He is leading me home.

As a young child, I knew Jesus loved me. I remember being taught prayers and praying at bedtime, praying for child things like helping me find my toy. I asked my mother, grandmother, and others questions as they came up. I had a Bible that I received on my second birthday. It was the old King James Version. I began reading it and grew to love it. I think I was around eight years old when I started reading it. You would wonder how an eight-year-old could understand the Bible that was written in old English, but I was hungry to hear and read His Word. I started to go to Sunday school, and there were scriptures above each of two Sunday school rooms in the sanctuary. I memorized them. At age twelve, I knelt and asked Jesus into my heart at a youth meeting, and I was baptized in water, in the lake, at age sixteen as a profession of my faith. I was very active in the church, teaching Sunday school, playing piano and singing, and being youth leader and choir leader.

I am grateful for the little church I attended and the teaching I received. I felt lots of love there. However, I grew up with church Christian teaching that was based on rules and judgment. I was taught that I had to be perfect and follow the rules and regulations, including how you must be at church every Sunday and evening and more if possible. Dancing, movies, television, playing cards, pierced ears, most jewellery were not allowed. A woman's dress had to be modest, and on and on. What I remember of those early days was that divorce was the worst "sin" that anyone could commit next to adultery, and adultery was the only reason for divorce. A girl was shunned if she became pregnant, which shamed many women. It did put the "fear" of God in me to not get pregnant because I knew that my family and my church and maybe the community would disown me. Women were monitored in ministry as men did the preaching. There was no equality. Women were to be submissive to their husbands, and so strong women with opinions were looked down on.

There were few families who had a divorce, and ours didn't have any until I was in my teens. So when divorce came into my life, I was massively confused. This shouldn't be happening, this is wrong. I am wrong. Finally, on my knees, I "told" God, "If I stay in this marriage, I will spiritually and physically die, and I can't imagine that would be Your will." It doesn't sound like a kind and loving Heavenly Father. I searched my heart and finally just gave in to let it happen. I thought I had tried everything, and still I was unhappy. I prayed, "God, if this is a mistake, then I will just have to make the mistake and go on." As the years went by, I came to understand marriage in its beauty, filled with love, honor, and respect.

In my case, I had a hardened heart, and my choice was divorce. My grandparents were married fifty years and my parents for seventy-two years. We cousins have divorced and are part of the statistic that says today approximately 50 percent of marriages end in divorce. I do not support divorce if you are just tired of the other person because vows are said as a promise of commitment to the other person. A marriage should be worked on because a relationship is work, and I think that if everyone did the work, then most marriages could be saved, mine included.

I wanted to attend seminary when I graduated high school, but my parents thought it wasn't advisable, as it was a distance away from them, and they were concerned that I might not have the right foods to eat and get into problems with the diabetes. Diabetes ruled. So instead, I went to work at a bank and soon got married.

There were a lot of transitions at that time in my life, and I became a Christian who struggled with the walk. I think now that I got bored, though I still prayed and read the Bible and attended church, I just didn't see any future excitement in my life. However, the Lord did speak to my heart about attending Bible School. I tossed the idea aside as my situation with a husband and baby and the purchase of a house; it just didn't seem possible. I now understand that sometimes when God speaks to us, He tells us of what is to come and it may not happen right now. We must be patient and wait for His timing. I did attend seminary but not until many years later. Long- distance education made it possible.

For the next ten years, I struggled with my salvation but also realized that the Bible teaches us to walk out our salvation. When divorce was inevitable, I really needed my church family. I think the little church was shaken to the core with the divorce announcement. We were the perfect couple. I felt ex-communicated from the church, as I was no longer allowed to be in the music, teaching, or any leadership position. Therefore, I stopped going and felt like I lost all my friends. I was very alone. The church had been my life, and now I was alone.

I continued to pray even more, I had a very active prayer life, and I believe God taught me how to pray. I have memories of great times with God in that difficult time.

I could tell more stories of His protection and grace toward me, even though I had hardened my heart. I was wandering aimlessly and making more and more mistakes, trying to fill the emptiness in my heart. I still struggled with my beliefs and my early teachings of the church. What are the correct teachings? There are so many unanswered questions.

I told myself that I didn't need a church, as that would only cause me more hurt and pain, but I attended a few for a short time, and when things got a little tough, I would leave. Then I met a woman. We were in a business class together for several months. We began talking, and I found out that she was a Christian. Under my breath, I said, "Here we go." She was a loving and caring person and became a trusted friend. She walked what she talked, and there was no pressure or judgment.

I met her family too and found them to be lovely people. As time went on, I was invited to her church, and I accepted. Each week, I felt lonely but renewed. The church was friendly and welcomed me. The teaching was awesome. It was similar but different than where I had been. I really felt loved there, and I didn't want to run away. I attended for the next two years and grew in confidence and spiritual commitment.

Then I moved to Edmonton. Soon, I met my husband. Neither of us had a church home, and both of us wanted one. When we discussed this, he laughed and said, "Let's go there," pointing right across the street from our apartment. So for the next seven years, we attended there. When we moved across the city, we also moved churches, which is where we attend now. A lot of healing has happened within us both. We have found a teaching that is not legalistic and full of laws. We have found a church that just loves people and with true biblical teaching without judgment.

There is a book I am reading called *Understanding the Whole Bible* by Johnathan Welton. It describes so much of what I have learned and understood in my personal walk. It is a great book to read. It talks about women in ministry, divorce, freedom in Christ, the old and new covenant, and how the Old Testament is history that we learn from and the New Testament is about our freedom. It is the New Covenant.

We have to understand the Bible in its cultural setting and how things have changed. God isn't the one who has caused the destruction of the world; we are, and we are now responsible to make good choices to improve our world. The heavens are the Lord's, and the world is ours. I believe it was a gift to us. There is much good in the world, and our choices sometimes cause distention and trouble. As I always said, I have lived the life, and now I read about it and learn about what I have lived. This book is doing that for me. Jesus is not about bondage; He is about breaking bondages. He is not about war and hatred; He is about love. He is not about destruction; He is about healing.

I think that some nonbelievers think that Christians must be perfect, or we are hypocritical. Legalistic Christian thinking is still in our world, and in my opinion, it does a lot of damage. It presents Christians as having to be perfect people. I am a Christian, and I am surely not perfect. I am on a life journey, learning, just like everyone else in this world. The difference is my belief in God and the example of Jesus Christ that I follow. What being a Christian means to me is that I have a relationship with God. He is my friend. He, like my school friend, never leaves me. I have turned away, like I did with my high school friend, but when I came back, she was right there to meet me like no time had come between us. This is how my relationship is with my God. I am not under judgment; I am under love. We are not under the law of the Old Testament; we are in the grace, freedom, and love of the New Testament. He is a gentle and kind Father. I am still learning and always will be.

Do you know your purpose? For me, it is simple. I am here to help others. My gift is as a counsellor and encourager. If my learning experiences can help someone else, then I will share. As a counsellor I am just a very small part of an influence on a client's life. That is a privilege and one I don't take lightly. Many other people will influence them too.

When I counsel others, I picture myself getting on the road with the client where they are at. It isn't my journey; it is theirs. I am simply here to guide and encourage. Maybe they have had a terrible experience and pain in church like I did, maybe they are struggling with an impending divorce or many other issues such as depression. Maybe there is no desire to talk about spiritual things. All is okay. I am always careful not to put my beliefs onto anyone else. I do respect individuals and where they are at in life. My story is mine, and theirs is theirs. There is no judgment.

On an Easter Sunday morning in 1993, at a sunrise service on top of a mountain in the beautiful Okanagan Valley in British Columbia, Canada, I surrendered my whole life to the Lord Jesus Christ. A new life began, and I started to focus in a new way on my life. I wanted to surrender to God's will. Life was not perfect, nor were my choices. I was as a baby spiritually, learning to breathe, crawl, and walk again. In fact, in some ways, life seemed to worsen as I learned to trust Jesus in the dark times.

The poem, "Footprints," has a great message, and so I enter it here. I have found its meaning to be so true. It was first written in 1936, and the author is unknown. I quote it:

One night I dreamed I was walking along the beach with the Lord.
Many scenes from my life flashed across the sky.

In each scene I noticed footprints in the sand.
Sometimes there were two sets of footprints,
other times there were one set of footprints.

This bothered me because I noticed
that during the low periods of my life,
when I was suffering from
anguish, sorrow or defeat,
I could see only one set of footprints.

So I said to the Lord,
"You promised me Lord,
that if I followed you,
you would walk with me always.
But I have noticed that during
the most trying periods of my life
there have only been one
set of footprints in the sand.
Why, when I needed you most,
you have not been there for me?"

The Lord replied,
"The times when you have
seen only one set of footprints,
is when I carried you."

I will continue with the last ten to twelve years. It has
been another kind of journey. Of course, I am not as
young as I once was and the years and diabetes are
taking a toll.

I was living in the beautiful province of British Columbia, Canada. Near to the ocean and the mountains that fed my spirit. I had many experiences there that are memorable both personal and professional. Working from home was lovely in some ways and very isolating in others. My private practice was called 'Make It Happen'. I rented an office at a business center for private work and meetings and travelled through the region visiting homes of families who have autistic children. I would meet with them and set up the program for their family. Personally, I had friends both from a church I was attending and a group of women that I met through a friend. We did lots of celebrating…everyone's birthday or any other celebration that came along. Lots of fun! And then, a contract came my way that changed my life's direction. I became a telephone counsellor for an employee assistance company in downtown Vancouver. After a year, the regional manager position in Edmonton came available, I applied and soon was on my way to Edmonton. I remember being disappointed that something like this hadn't happened in Vancouver as I saw myself living there for the rest of my life as I loved it so much. However, my two sons and a new adventure were waiting in Edmonton and so life in Alberta became mine. Leaving a life I had built in Vancouver was tough, but I looked forward to what God had in store for me in Alberta. Yes, cold and long winters. However, I soon met the man who would become my husband. Having my son close and being able to see him anytime was amazing. I had missed my children so much. I always hoped they would move to Vancouver but that didn't happen. I was regional manager for five years during which time my new husband had to have quadruple by-pass surgery and I had an accident where I broke my femur bone. These events were life changing for us. My career changed again as I felt I needed to step out of management and have less stress in my life. The company graciously hired me as a full time counsellor and when I left them after ten years, I opened my private practice 'Make Life Happen Counselling & Coaching'. During these years, we also had three deaths in our families. My husband's mother passed, my father passed and my husband's guardian child passed too. My mother who is now almost 96 years old is in a residence in Ontario and so I make a point of calling her often and visiting from time to time. Care giving a senior relative from a distance is amazing and stressful psychologically. Wanting to be there and not able to be is an emotional drain at times, but having a mother with me for all these years has been a tremendous blessing. You may be wondering about my younger son too as I haven't mentioned him. My greatest desire in returning to Edmonton was that I could be close to both my sons and mend any fences that were broken. My son made the decision to remain estranged from me.

The rivers my family and I have crossed have been difficult and yet strengthening. I believe the Lord walks with us as we put our foot into that river and believe as we swim to the other side with Him.

The Bible tells us we are never alone and that He will never leave us and I have certainly experienced that to be true. I also believe that we are given experiences to share with others and that is the main reason I am writing this book. I just want to share His goodness to me.

Most recently, my husband fell off the roof of our garage, while shingling it. He broke his wrist and his upper jaw. As a golfer, he wasn't impressed, but after finding out that he probably blacked out, he now has a pace maker to keep that heart ticking along correctly. Four surgeries later we are grateful for modern medicine. Without it, both of us, would have had a very short life. We wouldn't be here to tell the story.

Sometimes I say I should stop and just let the younger ones take over. They have more energy than me. But when Caleb in the Bible was eighty-five years old he said to God, "Give me a mountain to conquer" and God did. I feel the same. The mountains of this life and the rivers to cross are given to teach so we can learn to have faith in God. I believe and can say with the amazing teacher, Joyce Meyers, I can do whatever life gives me through Christ who strengthens me. Philippians 4:13. I can handle anything with Him when I let him be in charge.

And so, looking forward. What comes next in life I will only know when it happens. One thing that excites me and, that is in the planning, is the launch of this book. I had no idea what I was getting into when I said I was going to write a book, it is a long and rather arduous chore and I must say very enlightening. The clinical practice is doing well and we have a vacation planned in July. I love to wait in anticipation of what God has planned for me. For my older friends reading this book, please remember God has a plan, *always*. His planning never stops and His will for our lives doesn't change. He never gives up on us.

The Bible talks about a place that's called Heaven and many family members will one day meet me there. I come from a family of many generations of Christians. My grandfathers were lay preachers and spoke the gospel wherever they went. Many prayers were said for me. In my lifetime, if I have helped even one person to find hope, then I know I have succeeded.

Presently, above my desk I have a painting by Allissia S. It is a monarch butterfly sitting on a green leaf. There is a saying underneath the butterfly that says "Change. It is in changing that things find purpose." I love the change, I love the purpose and I love LIFE.

Chapter Eleven

THE REST OF THE STORY

"If a ploy brings joy, pursue it.
Where there's scope for hope, renew it.
If trouble's lurking, view it,
Then start working to subdue it.
If worry's worrying, shoo it.
If a job's worth doing, do it."

—By J.M. Robertson

In February, 2016, I added Self-Sabotage Coach to my counsellor tool kit. Our own personal truth is what we believe about ourselves. Is this limiting belief or believing we can achieve whatever we want to? We must find out where our deserve level is and then set new deserve levels as we achieve the last one. This is the healing that changes our personal truth about ourselves. I sure wish I had this training when I was young. My decisions and choices would have been very different.

Messages come at to us from many avenues, people, media, TV, books, radio, billboards, advertisements, and so on. This all starts with our parents who birthed us. However, we cannot blame our parents for our adult choices, nor can we blame our parents if we don't pick up the ball of life and heal our hurts. Our parents teach what they were taught and where I come from in my generation, psychology was a myth, mental illness was a shame, and what happened within a family stayed within the family.

In the midst of all the turmoil, part of what caused chaos is I moved residence twenty-six times. I lived in two new houses, rental houses, old houses, and the one I live in now was built the same year I was born, condo, apartments, mobile homes, and for six months in winter in a small twelve-foot trailer in a trailer park. I loved new starts, new community, and new experiences.

Someone once said to me that I didn't visit a place as a tourist; I visited to explore living there and usually chose the latter. My own thinking as a child was, if I ever get a chance to see the world, I will! When I had children, I felt that I had been stagnated, and the expectation of my family was that I would always live in that small town or close vicinity. My plan was to make sure my kids got to have many experiences, and moving was all a part of that thinking.

What I didn't realize at that time is how much children need stability in their life. My kids got tired of moving and rebelled. I hadn't looked at the whole picture, just a portion. After all, who makes the choice to move twenty-six times in their life? Who wants to do that? The good thing is you learn to travel light!

I have wonderful memories of the farm. It was a century farm, and it had been in our family for one hundred years when my father finally sold it. I loved playing outside as a child. I always had pets. A dog, cats, chickens, and turkeys. We had animals who grazed in the orchard by our house, cows and pigs mostly. I had a pet horse, when I was thirteen, that my father bought for me when I was in the hospital getting my tonsils removed. I think he felt sorry for me because I had spent so much time of my childhood ill and lots of time in the hospital. I called my horse, Mr. Ed. He was a white Shetland pony. I had great fun with him. He was spunky and full of mischief. He would run and buck in the pasture.

One day, when Dad and I were eating breakfast and looking out the window, we saw Ed's head come through the roof of the barn where he was housed. My father wasn't too pleased, as he had eaten his way through the roof. I think it must have taken him all night. There he was saying, "good morning" and looking proud of his mischief. I would dress him up in ribbon array and braid his tail. A saddle was too expensive for us to buy so bareback it was. Ed loved it, but he sure wanted to go where he wanted to go, and sometimes he would just stop and plant his feet.

I may have fallen off a few times but nothing serious, but if a man came near him to ride him, he didn't like that, and my father often ended up in a ditch or on the ground when he tried to tame this fellow. Oh, great fun I had with him.

I also had a dog named Mike. Mike was a German Shepherd, and Dad got him as company for me, as I was often alone on the farm after school until everyone else came home. I always felt protected with Mike nearby. We romped and explored and had a great time together. I taught him to jump through a Hula-Hoop, and he did it so well. I had hours and hours of fun with that dog.

And then I had a baby wild duck. A man had found it stranded and brought it to our farm to see if we would care for it. It became my pet. We had a watering trough for the cattle, and that became its home. We became great friends. I was a privileged farm girl, who had these wonderful experiences of being raised on a farm. Through the dark cloud came the rays of sunshine. My animal friends were the sunshine.

And then there were the rainbows. On the farm, you really make note of the weather. I loved to stand looking out the old screen door as the rain pelted down and the thunder and lightning filled the sky. I was never afraid of storms; I thought of them as God's way of speaking to the world. After the storm came the beautiful rainbow. I would go outside and look at it with wonderment. There was nothing more exciting than seeing a rainbow. My mother would tell me the story of Noah and the flood and how the rainbow is the sign from God that he will never flood the earth again. This brought peace and solace and an understanding that God does speak to the world in countless ways.

As a little girl, I loved to play mud pies. This was playing like I was in a kitchen, sitting on the ground mixing water and sand to make cookie dough. I would then put the dough in the oven (in the sun) to cook (dry). My mother is still horrified when I tell her I used to also eat them. No wonder I was given worm medicine, just in case! Heaps of fun.

When it was harvesttime, farmers would help farmers harvest the crops. Sometimes they would let me ride on the wagon from one location to another. My mother used to help with the hay harvest and told stories of finding snakes in the hay and hanging them on the fence. Yikes, that still gives me chills. The men harvested, and the women cooked meals and snacks and made sure there was always coffee or a drink delivered to the field every few hours. It was usually hot weather, and it was important the men didn't become dehydrated.

Mom and I used to go to the bush or the woods as we called it. Part of our farm was trees and had been there for hundreds of years. They all grew up wild. It was beautiful in the spring and summer. The wild flowers bloomed, and raspberries, gooseberries, and blackberries grew wild. I loved blackberries, and when I was pregnant with my first son, I told Mom I wish I had some blackberries. She took the time and energy to go to that same bush and get me some blackberries. Wow, did they taste good.

My grandmother always had a huge vegetable garden. When I was young, she would take me with her as she hoed and nurtured the plants. Sometimes I "helped" her harvest it too. We grandchildren had to get special permission and were always warned not to step on the fruit. Grandma used this as teaching moments so that when I had my own house, I was able to also garden and do a great job of it. Grandma was an awesome lady who lived to be one hundred years old. The memory of her home-baked cookies I will never forget. She gave me her recipe when I got married, and I made them too but never as good as hers. A little of this and a little more of that was how she gave recipes as she never measured anything. She was an awesome cook, and she had been a cook for a banker's family in Detroit in her young years.

We children always had a swing on the farm. There was a huge bush beside the tree where the rope was hung. One day, I went to go to the swing, and under it was a baby snake. It was a blowing atter, and it was so cute. However, my mom wouldn't let me play with it, as she always said where there is a baby there is a mother. We were quite used to seeing snakes, and at that age, I had no fear. In my teens, however, that changed when I came face-to-face with a huge rattle-snake. We think it likely floated down the creek that was swollen with water after spring rains, and then it had crawled up to our house and was coiled up, sleeping in the sun beside our porch. I came running out of the house and almost stepped on it. It sprung up and rattled, and I became very still. I was frozen. When I didn't move, it slowly uncoiled and slithered away. "I became terrified of snakes." I still don't like them and will avoid one at all cost.

MUSIC—MY OTHER PASSION

When I was a little girl, we only had a radio. I would hear my folks listening to country music or old-time music, as they called it, into the wee hours of the morning. My grandfather played the fiddle, and we kids would dance. Mother bought a piano, and I took lessons until I entered high school. I loved music. I loved the fact that I could make music.

At age twelve, our pastor's wife wanted to see if I could sing, and she taught me some songs, and I started to sing for the congregation. I later learned the accordion, and some of the young people played music together at church and events around the area. This was all just for fun, and never did we get any money, nor did we expect it.

My uncle, who was a railroad man, invited me to sing for the Christian Railroad Conference in Detroit, Michigan. I was around sixteen years old then, I believe. This is a cherished memory. We stayed in a motel, ate great food at the conference, and I played and sang all weekend. I got lots of attention, and I think I was paid a little token for my performance.

The piano I learned to play music on travelled with me until finally I had to let it go. I was moving so much that it was costly to be hauling a piano around. However, that was well after both my sons learned to play on it too.

When my sons were teenagers, their passion was music. Most of their spare time was spent playing and singing, and they were part of several bands. Later they travelled and toured before setting up their own business teaching children who were passionate about music too. My youngest son plays the violin, and so generation after generation, the music continues.

I used to get up very early in the morning and go downstairs to the radio just to listen to the Statler Brothers and other great Christian artists singing their praises to God. This was before anyone else was awake. However, they were soon awake, as it was hard to keep the volume down as I loved the music. The Oakridge Boys were a group that our church group went to hear perform. Our church youth leader had a Volkswagen bug. He had a couple of stools that he would put on the floor, and our group would pile into the car for the trip. We would sit on each other, on the stools, and if I remember right, one time we had twelve young people in that car. Boy, that would be against the law now, and it probably was unsafe, but it was the only way we had to get to the concert. I have many awesome memories of our youth group. Facebook is terrific, as we still connect from time to time.

I would be amiss if I didn't share a book that has inspired me; it's called *Rascal: Making a Difference by Becoming an Original Character* and was written by Chris Brady. I would encourage you to read it. Chris Brady's definition of a rascal is one I admire. "A rascal is a person who is willing to step out of line and pursue their own dream, not conform to the wishes of the masses." He goes on to say that rascals fear insignificance more than they fear peer pressure; they fear losing more than they fear change; they fear endless talk more than dangerous actions.

I am a rascal. I could have done anything I wanted with my life. I could have done good things or bad, or even ugly things, in this world. I had to learn to be a rascal. I had to learn my purpose for being in this world. I am an independent woman who had to learn to be interdependent in relationships. I am responsible for my life, and blaming others, as an adult, just isn't right! My faith has been a major part of my life story.

Being married and having a family bring with it big responsibility. It is hard being responsible for ourselves at times, but when one, two, or three little people become our responsibility, it can be overwhelming. With our decisions in life comes responsibility for the outcome, and becoming a parent is a decision you can never turn your back on or walk away from. It is our responsibility for a lifetime.

I learned that I am responsible for my own feelings. My feelings are mine. Someone else cannot make me feel anything. Yes, they can hurt my feelings, but I am the one who chooses what to feel. By that I mean one person can feel hurt in a situation, and another coming through the same experience can feel sad. Each person processes situations for themselves.

As my grandmother said, "I am determined." I became determined to change myself, to make myself a better person, to work through my regrets in life, and to be happy! My desire has been to help others on their journey. When a client comes into my office, I know that I am touching their life and helping them take one more step to freedom and their happiness. They learn very quickly that I cannot do the work for them; I am simply a guide as we walk together for a little while.

Chapter Twelve

CONCLUSION TODAY
AND TO BE CONTINUED

"Look back with pride on all you've accomplished,
look forward with excitement to
all the adventures ahead,
and just enjoy yourself-you have earned it!"

—Author unknown

"When a storm is coming, all
other birds seek shelter.
The Eagle alone, avoids the storm by flying above it.
So, in the storms of life…May
your heart soar as an eagle."

—Author unknown

As a child, I lived in a fantasy world. It was a wonderful place to be. I was raised as an only child, as my sister was older. I don't remember her much in my childhood. I spent most of my time alone playing with my pets.

Quite often on the farm, we had visitors who would come for Sunday dinner. My grandmother baked all day Saturday to prepare. Seldom did she know if anyone would come or who would come, but she was always prepared. Cousins or other kids would visit, and there would be playmates for a while.

I remember Christmas concerts at our little school when all the parents and families would come together to see the children perform the Christmas story and sing songs. Mom always made me special food and drink to replace the sugary ones that other kids had. Mom worked hard to provide for me so I didn't feel different from the other kids. I did, however, feel different, but I felt special.

Then came the Christmas concert at church. I always had a wonderful time there. We sang and played music, and usually I was in a play. There were lots of lines to memorize, and sometimes I forgot them. There was always a Christmas bag with an apple and orange and candy, which, for me, was replaced with a few coins. Usually, we received a little gift too. Great fun!

Christmas on the farm was unbelievable. Lots of excitement for this little girl. Dad would bring in a tree from the bush, and we would decorate it with a few simple decorations. I remember making paper chain links to put on the tree. They were wrapped round and round. On Christmas morning, Santa would have arrived. In my stocking, there was always fruit and several small toys and some socks. At the Christmas tree, there would be one larger gift.

The favorite one I remember was a telephone operator set. We had recently gotten the telephone put into our house, and when I went with Mom into town to pay the bill, I loved to watch the operator work. I decided then that I wanted to be a telephone operator. By the time I was old enough to work, those operator jobs were extinct, so that dream was gone with progression.

For Christmas dinnertime, we would go to my aunt's, and for suppertime, we would go to my grand-father's. Lovely turkey meals were served at both homes. There were lots of fun with cousins and aunts and uncles. The adults bought a gift for each child, so we walked away with lots of loot. What a fun day Christmas was! Awesome childhood memories!

As we got older, our Christmases changed because there were now too many people to meet at a house. It was decided that each family would have their own Christmas and that folks would get together over the holidays as they could. Life was becoming more complicated with my mother working out of the home and teenagers bringing boyfriends and girl-friends. All was good; however, we cousins started to drift apart as we got jobs in the city, married, and started our own families.

And so here it is, the good, the bad, and the ugly. This book has been many years in the making.

A client once asked me if I was going to write a book. I said yes but I don't have the format yet. She said, "You don't have the conclusion *yet*," and it was true. That statement remained with me. The conclusion will not truly be until I have passed from this world; meanwhile, the journey continues.

An unknown author said these wise words, "Everything in your life is a reflection of a choice you have made. If you want a different result, make a different choice."

All I can say is, I wonder what is next. There are always crossroads coming. That will never change. All we can do is make the choice and remain positive.

The butterfly has emerged and learned to fly! Come fly with me! Life is short, just a few years on this planet. The time passes quickly! My motto is, make the best of the experiences I have, learn from them, and teach others how to "make life happen."

"Happiness is a butterfly, which when pursued, is always just beyond your grasp, but which, if you will sit down quietly, may alight upon you" (Nathaniel Hawthorne).

This story will continue, the last chapter has not been fulfilled. Someday, somewhere, somehow, maybe my children will write a sequel.

Thank you for listening, for sharing, and for understanding. Until we meet again!

Bibliography

The Seven Principles for Marking Marriage Work

    John Gottman

Divorce, God's will?

    Stephen Gola

Helping Your Kids Cope with Divorce
the Sandcastles Way

    M. Gary Neuman

Inside the Minds of Angry and Controlling Men

    Lundy Bancroft

Rascal

    Chris Brady

The Five Love Languages

    Gary Chapman

Changes that Heal

    Cloud

The Courage to Heal

Ellen Bass and Laura David

Stop-Self-Sabotage

Pat Pearson

The Anger Workbook

Carter, Minirth

Why Does He Do That?

Lundy Bancroft

Understanding the Whole Bible

Johnathan Welton, Ph.D

http://www.hopedivorce.com—
Christians and divorce

http://www.domesticviolnce.com—[infor-
mation on resources in your area]

http://www.empoweringparents.
com—[estrangement]

http://www.sexualassault.ca—[sex-
ual assault information]

Voices from the Edge, a research report, Route One
Research Services, 2017, Alison Wheatley

Other Writings
by Eva L. Shaw

Mentoring Women Leaders [Book]
Sponsored by Womanition
Co-author (2015)
Womanition Magazine
October 2015 edition, Page 46
Divorce Magazine
February 2017 edition
http://www.divorcemagazine.com
http://www.marriage.com
[articles by Eva on marriage]
http://www.poemhunters.com
Eva's poetry
http://www.makelifehappen.info
[website]
http://www.evalshawtraining.com
[blog]

Contact information:
Eva L. Shaw is available at
eshaw@makelifehappen.info
Website: http://makelifehappen.info

Resources for Your Information

The "butterfly" quotes are taken from the Butterfly Web site and are from authors, philosophers, scientists, so-named.

Facebook: Bullying in Canada

http://www.mindyourmind.com

http://www.hopedivorce.com—Christians and divorce

http://www.domesticviolnce.com—[information on resources in your area]

http://www.empoweringparents.com

Sexual Assault Statistics in Canada

http://www.sexuaassault.ca

http://www.hopedivorce.com—Christians and divorce

http://www.domesticviolence.com—[information on resources in your area]

RAINN – Rape, Abuse, & incest National Network

National Sexual Assault Hotline 800-656.HOPE

An Open Letter to Child Sexual Abusers

Hawkins, Diane

Wilkepedia on Burnout

http://www.canadiandiabetesassociation.ca

About the Author

Eva L. Shaw earned a Doctorate of Philosophy and a master's degree in Christian Counselling from Covington Theological Seminary and a Bachelor of Science degree in nutrition from Donsbach University. She also has two certificates in general social work and child abuse from the University of Waterloo. Her thesis was called "Historic Female Sexual Abuse."

Ms. Shaw co-authored the book, *Mentoring Women Leaders,* and has written articles for the Womanition Magazine, Divorce Magazine, and marriage.com Web site. She has published poetry on poetryhunters.com, including an e-book. She is a member of the International Women's Leadership Association and was named as top woman executive. Her article, "Diabetics in the Workplace," is used in teaching student medical doctors and dentists just what it is like to live with diabetes. She has a training and information blog (evalshawtraining.com). She also sponsors the Wounded Warriors program for Canadian Military Veterans and a child in the Philippines through Compassion Canada.

Eva L. Shaw is a registered clinical counsellor and a self-sabotage coach. She was the first executive director of a new women's shelter and an employee assistance counsellor, including being a regional manager for ten years. Her curriculum vitae is unique and includes training and experience in a variety of issues. She is known as a relationship specialist. Eva and her husband, Warren, live in Edmonton, Alberta, Canada.

CPSIA information can be obtained
at www.ICGtesting.com
Printed in the USA
LVHW04s1155090718
583149LV00001B/17/P